D0592994

THE WINE GUY

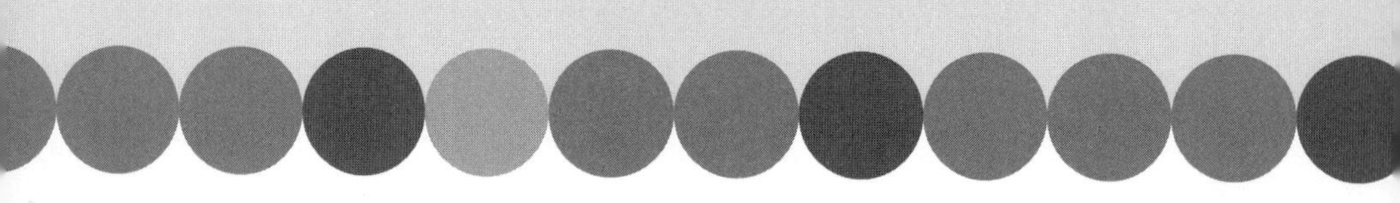

WILLIAM MORROW
An Imprint of HarperCollins*Publishers*

THE WINE GUY

EVERYTHING YOU WANT TO KNOW ABOUT BUYING AND ENJOYING WINE FROM SOMEONE WHO SELLS IT

ANDY BESCH
WITH ELLEN KAYE

 For information address HarperCollins Publishers Inc., 10 East 53rd Street, New York, NY 10022.

HarperCollins books may be purchased for educational, business, or sales promotional use. For information please write: Special Markets Department, HarperCollins Publishers Inc., 10 East 53rd Street, New York, NY 10022.

FIRST EDITION

Designed by William Ruoto

Printed on acid-free paper

Library of Congress Cataloging-in-Publication Data

Besch, Andy.
The wine guy : everything you want to know about buying and enjoying wine from someone who sells it / Andy Besch with Ellen Kaye.—1st ed.
p. cm.
ISBN 0-06-058299-5
1. Wine and wine making. I. Kaye, Ellen, 1954– II. Title.

TP548.B4157 2005
641.2'2—dc22 2005045709

ISBN-13: 978-0-06-058299-9

05 06 07 08 09 WBC/RRD 10 9 8 7 6 5 4 3 2 1

To our customers.

And to Chris and Bibi, who would have gotten a big kick out of this.

CONTENTS

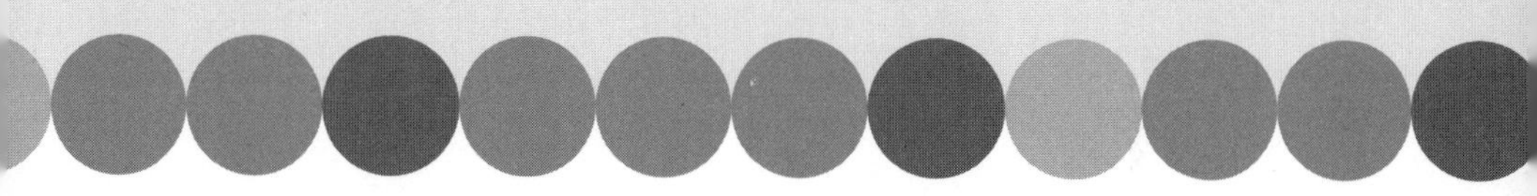

ACKNOWLEDGMENTS

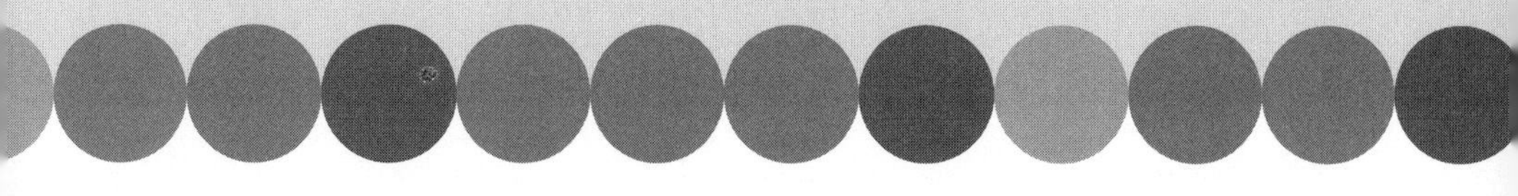

Many thanks to all the people whose brains we picked during this great adventure. The good news was that we got a book deal. But then reality hit, and we had to sit down and write. Fortunately, you were all there for us. So here's to our early readers, Doug Kaye, Mary Hall, Nancy Pierce, and Joe Igoe. A special toast to David "Sweet Lou" Bender, whose familiarity with both grape and grammar was invaluable. We raise a glass to Bill Bendelow for his patience with countless and sometimes inane questions, and for sharing his knowledge throughout. Cheers to our friend Leslie Schnur for making us believe this could happen, and for her guidance when it actually did. Salud to our posse at West Side Wine, Leo Rivera and Raymond Batista, for keeping things rolling while the book was being written, and for helping to make the business the success it is today.

We are extremely grateful to our crack editor, Harriet Bell, for getting us started and for making us make this book the best it could be. You were so right! A big thank you to our wonderful agent, Susan Ginsburg, whose encouragement, advice, and words of wisdom always came at just the right time.

Many, many thanks to our family for their support and enthusiasm. We love you all.

And last, but not least, thanks to winemakers everywhere for your sweat, tenacity, and creativity, and for the inspiration and joy that comes from the glass.

INTRODUCTION

WELCOME TO MY WORLD OF WINE

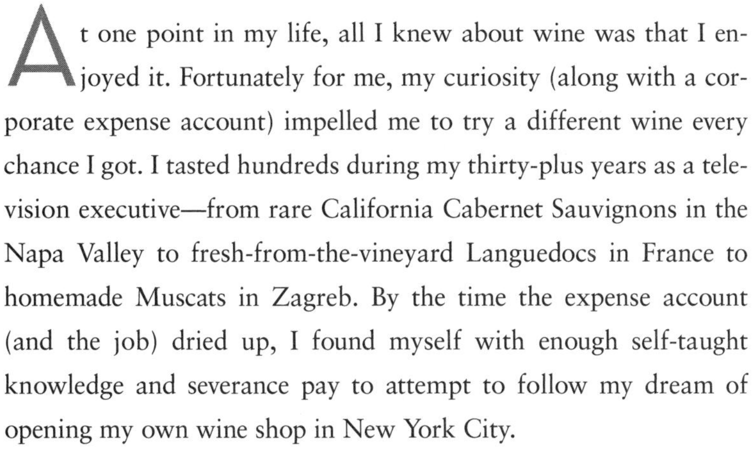

At one point in my life, all I knew about wine was that I enjoyed it. Fortunately for me, my curiosity (along with a corporate expense account) impelled me to try a different wine every chance I got. I tasted hundreds during my thirty-plus years as a television executive—from rare California Cabernet Sauvignons in the Napa Valley to fresh-from-the-vineyard Languedocs in France to homemade Muscats in Zagreb. By the time the expense account (and the job) dried up, I found myself with enough self-taught knowledge and severance pay to attempt to follow my dream of opening my own wine shop in New York City.

My wife, Ellen, and I began to walk the streets of Manhattan searching for the perfect spot. We walked, and walked, and then walked some more. In a stroke of luck, a location became available just two blocks from our home on the Upper West Side. It was a wreck of a liquor store, but the opportunity was too good to pass up.

I was scared to death. I knew my wines pretty well, but absolutely nothing about owning my own business. Where to start? I figured the best thing to do was to create my dream store—the one

I'd wanted in the neighborhood when I was a Saturday wine shopper. Out went the Johnnie Walker clock on the wall, the layers of dust on the shelves, the faded cardboard Santas in the windows. In went the new hardwood floors, the soft lighting, and a great sound system. I wanted a calm, welcoming atmosphere, with aisles wide enough for baby strollers and a tub of treats for the local canine population.

Next, and most important, came changes in the inventory. Out went the boxes of Almaden Mountain Chablis, the straw-covered jugs of Chianti, and the half-pints of Georgi vodka. I proceeded to stock the shelves with hundreds of my own hand-picked favorites, many from small little-known producers. In went Carmenieres from Chile, Malbécs from Argentina, Grüner Veltliners from Austria, Gewürztraminers from Tasmania, Puglian reds, Gallician whites, Greek rosés—offbeat, delicious wines from all over the world.

Such a nice-looking place, such a variety of good, affordable treasures. West Side Wine was ready to take the neighborhood by storm.

But once behind the counter, I soon realized that my customers and I were not on the same wavelength. To my astonishment, they were not bowled over by my amazing selection! No one even glanced at my basket of French Picpoul. Not a soul was drawn to my shelf of Dãos and Douros from Portugal. On the contrary, many were disappointed not to find their old reliables. *Where's my Turning Leaf Merlot? What happened to my Lindeman Chardonnay? How come you don't have my Woodbridge Cabernet? What, no Carlo Rossi?*

Change unnerved a lot of them. On my third day in business one woman commented, "You've changed the store."

"Why, yes I have," I proudly replied.

She paused, looked me in the eye, and said, "I hate change." Then she walked out, never to return.

Those customers who were willing to try something different often agonized over choices. Some, once convinced to try something new, never strayed from *that* selection, week after week. Most seemed completely lost.

I had a mission. My customers desperately needed the wine-buying process to be less painful and more rewarding, and I needed to sell more wine. I had to come up with an easy way for them to become confident enough to take advantage of this sea of new choices, without relying on the familiarity of a brand name or the lure of a gimmicky label.

So I began to walk customers through a series of questions designed to get them accustomed to thinking more about what they wanted in a wine. We talked body, grapes, flavors, styles, and meals. We talked about wines they had tried and liked, and wines they had tried and didn't like. I got them to articulate their preferences in words we both understood. The final step was to convince them to be a bit daring and take a chance on some of the many wines they had never tried before, but that I knew they would like.

At first I met a lot of resistance. Many customers didn't want to be challenged or questioned—they just wanted a bottle of wine. But now most of my regular customers know how to communicate their needs so I or a member of my staff can help them find the perfect bottle for any occasion. Many feel bold and confident enough to choose on their own, venturing fearlessly into unknown territory—Sardinia, Jumilla, Pic St-Loup, Wachau, Margaret River, Marlborough, and many other wine-making regions all over the world, where they've been rewarded with high quality, tremendous variety, and great values.

My approach can work for you, too. Take advantage of what I've learned from listening to the thousands of customers who have come through my door. Let me be your Wine Guy. I will provide personal guidance, mixed with just enough practical information to help you acquire the one and only skill you really need—the ability to identify and articulate your own tastes in wine. I'll be by your side as you taste your way to the point where you're confident enough to step into any wine store and walk away with a bottle that's perfect for you every time.

The good news is that finding the right bottle is now easier than ever before. We live in a brave new wine world, one in which the old rules no longer apply. Consumption is up, and that's good news for everybody. Wine producers, recognizing the growing thirst for immediately consumable everyday wines, are rising to the challenge. Everyone is in on the effort to make wine less elitist and more accessible. More high-end producers are creating affordable lines without sacrificing quality, bargain imports are pouring in from countries all over the world, and winemaking techniques everywhere have improved, which means there are more consumer-friendly choices. Never before has there been such variety, such interesting options, and such good value when it comes to wine.

Perhaps you're thinking, "Well, that doesn't sound so easy. More choices to confuse me? More bottles on the shelves to intimidate me? More things I have to learn about?"

True, with so much choice out there, learning about wine *is* a whole new ball game, but not in the way you probably think. The old-school way of gaining a wine education meant straining to commit labels and vintages to memory, hoping to recall them the next time you found yourself searching the wine store shelves or perusing a menu. But today there's no way you could possibly know about everything that's out there. Nor should you. Besides, wine is a living, evolving product, and it's changing faster now than ever before.

What you do need to know is how to get in touch with your own tastes and how to establish a good relationship with the people who sell you wine. If they are good (and I'll tell you how to find those who are), they are spending their days tasting all those new, exciting wines, so they can pass that knowledge on to you. As long as you effectively communicate your wine preferences, there is absolutely no excuse for you ever to walk out of a store or restaurant without choosing something you can be confident you'll enjoy, and at the same time is *new to you.*

Your job is to read a little and taste a lot of wine. The process should be both enjoyable and fruitful, not a chore. It's all about the pleasures of wine, after all. And in this quest, getting there is more than half the fun.

THE WINE GUY

CHAPTER ONE

DISCOVERING THE WINE LOVER WITHIN

Why do so many people act as though picking out a bottle of wine is worse than going to the dentist? And why do others barely give it a thought at all, relegating it to a dull routine?

It's because we think we have to "know about" a wine to take a chance on it. Well, guess what? You probably know more than you realize. It's simply a matter of tapping into the wine lover within, respecting and remembering your own opinions, and letting them lead the way.

With snooty sommeliers, reference books the size of world atlases, all that goofy wine lingo, and the sheer volume of choices out there, selecting a bottle is a situation that might scare off even the boldest among us. Relax. Learning about wine simply means figuring out what you like.

Learning about wine is, like bike riding and sex, best achieved by doing, which in this case means tasting. The learning actually starts even before you pop that first cork. It all begins with attitude. The way we mentally approach the wine-buying process can be the key to opening ourselves up to a whole new level of enjoyment. It's the first and most important step toward making the entire experience fun, easy, and rewarding.

When you shop for clothes, you probably breeze through the racks, knowing right away what appeals to you and what you wouldn't be caught dead in. In the supermarket, you select food based on what you're craving at the moment or what you think you'll want in the fridge tomorrow. Do you shop for wine the same way?

Probably not. Okay, so with clothes you can get a free preview in the dressing room. With wine, there is a cost to trying something on, but unless you've spent more than a few bucks, it's minimal. If you hate the wine, chuck it! And by the time you finish reading this book, the risk of making a disappointing purchase will be even lower. You'll be making educated choices based on taste—just like breezing through those clothes racks.

With food, you can usually figure out what a brand is going to taste like, even if you've never tried it before, because you can compare your choice to other foods you like. Guess what? It's the same with wine.

Shopping for wine should be almost as much fun as drinking it. Today there are many good choices in the affordable range of $10 to $15. And there is always something new to try, so you can't complain of boredom.

It's time to start looking at wine, and the wine-buying process, in a whole new way. Forget those misconceptions, fears, inhibitions, or habits that are holding you back. Perhaps some of the following scenarios will sound familiar to you.

One Saturday we were having a Burgundy tasting in the store. I watched as François, the winery rep, poured a sample for a young woman with a yoga mat rolled up under her arm. She took a sip and wrinkled her nose.

"You don't like it?" asked François.

She looked embarrassed. "Well, I don't really care for it, but then I don't really know anything about wine. It's probably very good!"

More often what I hear is "I know a good wine when I taste it." Well, that's fine. As long as by "good" you mean good by your own standards.

Your palate is your palate, and no one else's. All you really need to know is if a wine appeals to *you* or not. End of story.

When it comes to spending money on wine, people sometimes seem to think that they have to spend more than necessary. In fact I often sense that, when asked how much they want to spend on a bottle, customers end up blurting out a number even higher than the one they originally had in mind!

Mark, a regular, came in looking for a $30 bottle of California Cabernet to bring to a dinner party.

"Is there any magic in that number?" I asked. "Would you consider one from Australia for around $15?"

"Is it any good?"

I bit my tongue and guaranteed Mark that he would be a very popular guest, in fact the hit of the party, with that bottle.

On the other end of the spectrum was Cathy, who shuffled in on a Friday evening, burdened with laptop and briefcase and balancing a pizza box on one arm.

"I need a bottle of red," she sighed. "It doesn't have to be good . . . it's just for me."

My heart went out to her. Where was her self-esteem? Then I realized what Cathy was really saying. She didn't want anything expensive. She was, like Mark, mistakenly equating price with quality.

In today's wine world, price and quality have less and less to do with each other. Good everyday wines from just about every country are emerging as affordable luxuries.

So what makes some wines more expensive than others? Look at it this way: when you buy a home, you pay more to live in a fancier neighborhood. The same goes for grape growers. Napa Valley real estate is pricier than land in Rioja, Spain. As a wine consumer, you're paying for that. Wages in Oregon versus wages in Santiago, Chile? You're paying for that, too. Remember Economics 101, day one? Supply and demand? The less there is, the more it costs and the more precious it becomes (if it's good). You're paying for that preciousness. And then there's the hype factor attached to wines blessed with high ratings from the "experts." *Ka-ching!*

The distance between the vineyard and your dining room table can affect price as well. French wines are less expensive in New York than in California. On the other hand, California wines coveted by New Jerseyans line supermarket aisles in Van Nuys at ridiculously low prices. So remember that what you're shelling out is covering some guy's expenses for taxes, middlemen, packaging, marketing, and transportation, in addition to what it costs him to make the wine. And it's not necessarily buying you a better bottle.

Then there are those who shop till they drop, like the guy who showed up at our door in shorts and hiking boots, sweat dripping off his forehead.

"Do you carry Cakebread Cabernet?" he panted, as he leaned on the counter and tried to catch his breath.

"I don't, but what I *do* have is . . ."

He was already out the door. He had probably enjoyed that particular Cabernet in a restaurant. Maybe he wanted to pick up a bottle to serve to dinner guests that night or to share with his new girlfriend. He didn't give me the chance to warn him that if he kept running around looking for that wine, there might not be dinner for his guests, or that his girlfriend might be asleep by the time he got home.

On the same note, a couple pushing a double stroller came in looking for a particular $3 red from Campagna.

"Don't tell me," I said. "Let me guess. You shared that bottle on a hillside terrace one steamy August afternoon in Positano or Amalfi, on your honeymoon."

"How did you know?" they asked with incredulity, as the husband wiped off two pacifiers and shoved them into the crying babies' mouths.

I hear this all the time—people seeking a memorable bottle they can't get out of their head.

What the twins' parents, along with hiker-boy, don't know is that they probably would not be able to find the particular wines they were seeking in any store. It's unlikely that $3 Campagna red is even exported. And Cakebread Cabernet is one of the many wines that are "allocated," which means that since only a small amount is produced, distribution is limited. Restaurants usually get first dibs on buying, and sometimes winemakers don't even allow their wines to be sold in retail outlets. Rather than wasting time on a disappointing and frustrating experience, try a new wine and make new memories. There are thousands of special bottles awaiting you.

From the day I opened West Side Wine, Franny would come in to pick up a bottle of the same Pinot Grigio, week in, week out. One day, after we got to know each other a bit, I finally spoke up.

"Franny," I began, "what did you have for dinner last night?"

"Pot roast," she answered.

"And the night before?" I continued.

Franny thought for a moment. "Spaghetti, I think." Her brow furrowed quizzically.

"What are you planning for tonight?"

"Chinese takeout. Why are you asking me this?"

I proceeded to explain to Franny that she was in a wine rut. She wouldn't eat the same meal day in, day out, so why would she buy the same wine every time she came in? Wine isn't like toothpaste or laundry detergent, where you find your favorite brand and stick with it for life. There are thousands of different wine choices out there, from all over the world, made from lots of different grapes, and in all price ranges. Imagine what you are missing!

This isn't to say that no one should ever drink the same wine twice. When you find a wine you like, you *will* want to enjoy it again. And that's fine, as long as it's thrown into the mix, and doesn't become your one and only.

One summer evening I overheard a conversation between two young women as they cruised the aisles.

"Do you see anything you've heard of?" one whispered to the other.

"Not really. What should we do?" the other responded, wringing her hands.

Where do you hear about the wines you buy? Advertisements? All that means is that it's produced at a volume that justifies the marketing expenditure—not that it's necessarily one of the best in its price range. And if you go by only the recommendations of friends, relatives, or journalists? That's okay to a point, but only if you know what their recommendations are based on. Are their tastes similar to yours? Do you consistently agree on what's good? The tastes of others may not suit your own.

This goes as well for the guy who came in with his Palm Pilot loaded with the names of all the 2002 California Chardonnays that were rated by an "expert" 90 or above, determined to find something, *anything*, that was on that list. He was the type who liked to do his homework, and he was trusting the experts to provide him with all the information. But the ratings are based on *their* opinion, *their* taste. And if he insists on blindly following along, he's probably spending far more than necessary, because as soon as a wine is given a high rating, the price usually goes up.

There are thousands of wines that are never even considered by those who rate them. Winemakers from all over the world send their wines to publications such as *Wine Spectator* and Robert Parker's *The Wine Advocate* hoping that (a) their wine will be tasted and (b) it will receive a high rating that can be useful in marketing. The first part is tough enough. There are simply too many wines out there for even the most ambitious publications to evaluate. The absence of a rating doesn't mean the wine is bad. In fact, it doesn't mean anything. There's no need to clutter your brain with that type of information anyway. Make room for your own opinions. The only rating you should consider is the one you assign after *you* have tasted.

Then there are the guys who refuse to ask for help. And I say guys because it usually *is* guys. As with driving directions, women seem to be more likely than men to ask for wine help.

I have one thing to say to those guys: independence is not always a good thing. Like it or not, whether at a retail store or in a restaurant you are already paying for help, so get your money's worth. There's no shame in asking for information, recommendations, or help. In fact, asking for help can be the key to getting wines you'll enjoy.

Our friend Leslie was adamant about one thing: she hated Chardonnay. She held such a grudge that I couldn't resist the temptation of putting her to the test, so I slipped a white Burgundy into her fridge. She loved it. Little did she suspect that it was made from the Chardonnay grape.

My cousin Jeffrey said he hated Merlot.

"You must despise those lush, plump St-Emilions," I told him.

"Are you kidding? Those are great!"

"Huh. I just assumed . . . 'cause you know they're made mostly from the Merlot grape."

THE WINE GUY'S CREDO

Treat yourself.

Trust your own tastes.

Remember to remember.

Look for novelty and adventure at any given opportunity.

Keep an open mind.

Seek by quality, not by price.

Speak up. Ask for help.

Make new memories.

Never walk away empty-handed. Embrace choice!

Relax. It's just a beverage.

Don't let preconceived notions get in your way. Keeping an open mind (along with an open mouth) is an essential part of the learning process. You will be surprised at what you discover.

Recognize yourself in any of these people? I know I do. I recognize myself before I became the Wine Guy. Believe me, you're not alone. But it's time to say good-bye to those old wine-buying habits and approach wine from an entirely new perspective.

CHAPTER TWO

THE ART OF TASTING

I used to roll my eyes at people in restaurants who make a big deal out of tasting their wine. The swirling, the sniffing, the slurping—*oh please*, I would think. Then I started going to industry tastings, where I'd find myself surrounded by whole *rooms* full of people twirling, snorting, gargling, and spitting. What a scene! At first it was hard to keep a straight face, but now that I'm the Wine Guy, I've become one of them.

When we talk about wine, we talk in terms of flavor, which is a combination of taste, smell, and touch. To discern flavor in wine you need to call on your mouth, your nose, and even your eyes. (Forget about your ears—all wine sounds the same.) Your senses of taste, smell, touch, and sight send information to your brain, where it will be processed and stored for later recall.

Remember, the goal here is to identify and articulate flavor. There is a certain simple yet important routine you need to go through as you first taste a wine in order to get the information you'll need. Knowing how to use your senses, understanding what each of them brings to the experience of enjoying wine, and knowing how to maximize their powers will make the process of identifying your wine preferences a whole lot easier.

Serve it, see it, swirl it, smell it, sip it. It's that simple.

But you shouldn't be just sitting there reading about how to taste—you need to jump right in and do it! Open a bottle of wine, any bottle, and follow along.

SERVE IT

The amount of wine you pour into a glass affects the way it tastes. You and your wine need enough breathing room—you to be able to later swirl and sniff, and your wine to aerate. Aeration means giving the wine contact with oxygen, which at this point is a good thing, as the oxygen will release the wine's odors and bring it to life. Some of those poor babies have been locked up in steel tanks, oak barrels, and then the bottle for some time. Let them stretch!

If you're just sampling, pour enough for one very large gulp. Make sure you'll have plenty for a nice, healthy mouthful, because you're going to get your entire mouth into the act. If you want more than just a taste, fill the glass half full. Don't overpour—wineglasses are not designed to be filled to the rim. You can always have another glass.

SEE IT

Once the wine is poured, hold the glass up to the light and look at its color. Where a wine sits on the color palette is a heads-up for the rest of your senses. Once you start to associate colors with particular flavors, that first glance at a wine in the glass will trigger your anticipation, preparing your taste buds for the experience ahead.

The thicker the skins of the grapes, the richer the color of the wine, and the deeper the flavor. In general, the lighter the color, the lighter the wine. A Beaujolais made with Gamay grapes looks and tastes lighter than a Bordeaux, which is made with thicker-skinned Cabernet Sauvignon, Cabernet Franc, and Merlot grapes. A Pinot Grigio looks lighter than a California Chardonnay, and tastes lighter as well. Think of the color and taste differences between a blackberry and a strawberry. One is darker than the other by nature, yet each has its own level of richness and flavor.

The juice of most grapes, regardless of the color of their skins, is white when the grapes are crushed. During the fermentation process, the juice is left to soak, or macerate, with the skins to extract their color. The amount of time the crushed grapes and skins are in contact with each other determines the depth of color of the wine. Take a rosé, for example. A rosé can be made from very dark-skinned grapes, such as Cabernet or Merlot, yet rosés are always light in color, because the juice is separated from the skins within a few days, or even a few hours, as opposed to weeks into the fermentation process.

Color can also provide clues about age, alcohol content, and body. But for now, your primary focus should be the basic visual cue your eyes send to your mouth.

Just as you use your eyes to tell you how good a wine looks, you should also rely on your sight to warn you of a wine gone bad. Up until the point where the wine is uncorked and poured into the glass, oxygen is the enemy, as it causes chemical changes that may make the wine go flat and stale. This is called oxidation. You can tell by sight if a wine is oxidized by the funky color. Relatively young reds, which are normally bright, vivid, and rich, take on a brownish, orangey hue, resembling brackish water from a rusty pipe. With white wine, oxidation is a little tougher to detect, but if there's an unnatural yellow-orange cast, your antennas should go up. Since you will be using almost all of your senses, don't jump to conclusions and dump the wine right away. You'll want to smell and taste it thoroughly before passing final judgment. Sometimes this type of coloring is simply a result of the natural aging process.

SWIRL IT

Although the wine world is loaded with pretensions, swirling the wine in a glass before smelling or tasting it isn't one of them. On the contrary, it's a necessity. While oxygen is wine's enemy while it's in the bottle, once the wine is poured oxygen becomes its friend. Swishing the wine around vigorously in the glass, three or four times, allows as much of the wine as possible to make direct contact with the air around it, which in turn releases as much aroma as possible into the air that you're about to sniff. Your glass should be big enough to swirl without mishap while holding on to the base or the stem, but until you perfect your technique, you may want to stick to table-anchored swirling. Keeping the base of the glass on the table and pushing it around steadily in a small circle a few times will do the trick.

SMELL IT

After swirling, you sniff the wine. And don't just take a dainty little sniff at the edge of the glass. Get into it. Stick your nose down into that glass as far as it will go. Fill your nostrils with the bouquet. Then back up a little and let the odors come to you from a few inches away, to experience how the wine interacts with all that air outside the glass. Take as many inhalations as it takes to send advance information to your mouth, and also to your brain, where the aromas you detect will be linked to the countless flavors stored in your memory bank.

When it comes to identifying flavor, your nose is actually more important than your mouth. Flavor is made up of about 75 percent odor and 25 percent taste and touch. Our sense of smell is said to be about a thousand times more sensitive than our sense of taste.

Don't underestimate your own nose. It will prepare your mouth by whetting your appetite for the experience ahead. Remember salivating when you smelled Mom's apple pie in the oven or McDonald's French fries in the takeout bag? It's the same deal here. Your nose primes your taste buds by giving your brain a preview of the flavor to come.

Smell plays a large role in sensory memory. When you take a whiff, you're committing to memory something about that experience, and your nose has *great* memory. As a matter of fact, odor memory is kept longer than any other sensory memory. Your nose cues your memory to recall flavors that you do or don't like all the time, every day, basing its cues on past experiences.

Although you'll usually relate a wine's aroma to other edible or potable substances, it sometimes may evoke a strange association in your mind—perhaps a person, place, or inanimate object. Does it bring your Aunt Ida to mind, or make you think of your first set of wheels? That's your sensory memory going to work. You probably will eventually figure out the connection. Did Aunt Ida wear a floral perfume? Did that new car smell of leather? Both those aromas can be detected in some wines.

Also put your sense of smell to work if you suspect a wine has become oxidized. An oxidized wine will lose its fresh, fruity aroma and will give off a stale odor, eventually coming off as vinegar-like. Another potential problem that can be uncovered by your nose is cork taint, which happens when the wine comes in contact with a "diseased" cork. It's estimated that 2 to 7 percent of wine produced today becomes "corked." You'll know it by its musty, moldy, damp basement smell when you find it.

SIP IT

Your first taste should be a big, healthy mouthful, more than a sip. Expose the entire surface of your mouth to the wine, giving all your receptors a chance to do their thing. There are approximately ten thousand taste buds in your mouth, each made up of somewhere between 50 and 150 receptor cells, so you do the math. And those taste buds are all over the place—on the tip, sides, and back of the tongue, as well as on the palate, pharynx, and larynx. If you taste with just the tip of your tongue, you're not using everything you've got, making the task that much more difficult.

Gently swish the wine around in your mouth. Make sure every part of your mouth gets a chance to do its job. Suck in a little air through your lips to make the wine bubble in your mouth. Again, air helps release the flavor.

You're putting your sense of taste and your sense of touch to work simultaneously when you sip. Pay attention to the wine's "mouthfeel"—literally the way it feels inside your mouth.

Although you may be tempted, don't gulp it down right away. Let the wine stay in there for a few seconds. There are no second chances to take that first sip.

Have you ever witnessed some wine tasters spitting into buckets after they taste? After learning the hard way at my first professional wine tasting, I now do it all the time, since I often taste a lot of wines in one sitting and really don't want to get drunk. (I'm still perfecting the art of the no-splash spit.) But unless you are sampling lots of wines at once, I don't recommend spitting, as it may cause you to miss a chance to get more information from your taste buds. There are actually taste buds on the upper third of the esophagus, which allow you to taste food as it is being swallowed.

As you swallow the wine, note the "finish"—how the wine tastes after it goes down your throat. Is the wine equally as pleasurable from beginning to end? Some wines start out with a bang and end with a whimper; some start out soft and smooth, yet end with a bite—all from one sip!

If you suspect a problem with the wine from what you've seen and smelled, what does your mouth say? An oxidized wine will taste flat or sherry-like, and the musty, moldy odor of a wine suffering from cork taint will be obvious.

Your mouth will give you the answer to the one really important question: do you like the wine? A yes or no answer will suffice, at least as your immediate response.

That first sip helps determine your wine likes and dislikes, because at this point your mouth is unencumbered and fresh. A world of flavors comes from that first contact. Of course, you will get another chance with those second, third, and fourth sips. Some wines may take a few sips to get used to them. And you'll see that wine changes as it sits in the glass and is exposed to air. Good wines improve over time, great ones flourish, and some just collapse and die. But no sip is as telling as *numero uno*. So pay attention.

CHAPTER THREE

WHEN WE TALK ABOUT WINE

The counter at West Side Wine has become a modern-day cracker barrel, where folks stop in to talk about anything and everything from sports to politics to theater to music. The only subject that seems to be a verbal challenge for some of them is wine.

On one particular afternoon we conducted a taste test. I was pouring a Gewürztraminer and a Cabernet Franc, both wines that have very distinct flavor characteristics. We asked everyone who stopped by to tell us what the wines tasted like to them. People hemmed and hawed. Even when reassured that there were no right or wrong answers, they hesitated.

"Smooth?" ventured one brave woman.

"Okay," I answered. But what does it taste *like*?"

"I think the Gewürztraminer is kind of sweet," a guy suggested. "Right?"

"Can you find any other words to describe what you taste?" I prompted.

Silence.

I rest my case. When asked to describe the types of wines that you like, what's the first thing you say, other than perhaps "red" or "white"? If you are like most of my new customers, the words "sweet," "dry," or "smooth" immediately come into play, once you feel comfortable enough to speak up. In fact, I find that most people can describe wines *only* in those terms. That might be helpful—but only if we had a way to be certain we were both on the same page when it came to the meaning of those words.

THE SWEET LOWDOWN 

Let's start with the word "sweet." In the wine world, for the most part, the only wines that are truly designated as sweet are dessert wines, like Sauternes and Muscats. Most sweet wines are made from super-ripe grapes that have been allowed to stay on the vine longer than usual. Have you ever bitten into a table grape that was sitting around in a bowl for too long? Sugar rush! It's the same with wine grapes. As they "rot" their sugars increase, to the point that when the fermentation process (which turns sugar into alcohol) is complete there is so much leftover, or residual, sugar present that the only result can be a sweet wine.

Most wines can technically be considered to be some degree of dry, from bone dry to off dry to medium dry. In these wines, virtually all the sugar in the grapes is converted to alcohol during the fermentation process. So what makes some of them taste sweet? The perception of sweetness can come from a number of factors, such as the fruity flavor that results from the natural fruit extracts, which our senses associate with sweetness. Alcohol itself can produce a sense of sweetness. Certain types of oak found in barrels used for fermentation or aging can also make a wine taste somewhat sweet.

SMOOTH OPERATORS 

Lots of customers tell me they're looking for "something smooth." Another word I hear a lot is "sour," usually in the context of "I can't stand sour wines." While those words can have a number of meanings, my guess is that people are referring to a wine's **acidity**. Acidity is a natural quality that comes from the growing and fermentation processes, as well as from the nature of the grapes themselves. Geography plays a big role here: the cooler the climate, the more acidic the grape.

When the acidity level of a wine is perfectly balanced with the flavor of the fruit, the result is magic. Balance is what gives a good wine its character. In fruity wines, like Zinfandels or Chardonnays, acid can help to counterbalance the perception of sweetness, like squeezing fresh lemon juice over a bowl of ripe berries to bring out their flavor. In less fruity wines, like Sauvignon Blancs or Sangioveses, a certain level of acidity is necessary to bring the fruit to life.

Acidity shouldn't be detectible as a taste. In a white wine, acid should come across as a crisp, sharp, zingy quality, and sometimes even as a sense of effervescence, without the wine being actually bubbly. Acidity is what makes a white wine refreshing. In fruity red wines, acidity brings out the brightness and liveliness in the grapes, keeping the wine from being too jammy or flat. An acidic quality actually works very well when paired with rich, high-fat, or fried foods, as it will cut through the heaviness. Think of how nicely malt vinegar goes with fish and chips, or how a salad with a vinaigrette dressing complements fettuccine Alfredo.

Obviously, some wines may taste zingier or crisper or brighter than others, but they should never taste "sour." Wines that taste too acidic are often simply not good wines, or perhaps have been made with underripe fruit, or may be in need of further aging.

Sometimes when people use the word "smooth," as well as the term "soft," they're actually attempting to steer clear of yet another characteristic of some wines. Do you ever get that puckery feeling after sipping some red wines? That's not acidity, nor is it dryness. It's the **tannins**. Tannins are natural chemical compounds found in the seeds, stems, and skins of red grapes, as well as in new oak barrels used in the aging process. The level of tannins is determined by the thickness of the skins (the thicker the skin, the more tannic the wine) and the amount of contact the juices have with the crushed grapes.

Tannins in wine can be good or bad. At moderate levels, they produce a luxurious, creamy-textured feeling in your mouth. But if they're too pronounced, it's a sign that the wine is not ready to drink. During the aging process, tannins serve to soften the wine as a whole, while their own "puckery" quality diminishes. It's too late to do anything about an overly tannic bottle you've already opened, which probably wasn't meant to be drunk right away. But if you like everything else about that wine, and can get your hands on more of it, do so and put it away for a year or two. It will age and mellow out quite nicely.

THE BALANCING ACT

Even though they may not know it, what my customers are usually talking about when they use these somewhat vague terms is *balance*. Acidity, fruit, alcohol, tannins, and sweetness are all part of what make up a wine's balance. When a wine is well balanced, no one of these elements will overpower another. However, each wine has its own unique style, so within each there is a unique, "correct" balance.

Just because a wine is well balanced, there's no guarantee you'll like it. What may be right for the wine could be wrong for the taster. There will be certain styles that appeal to you more than others do.

If you are not sure how all of these elements of balance come across, try some wines that are extreme examples of the characteristics we've been considering. The sensations will be quite obvious. There is no need to sample them all—concentrate on the characteristics you're not sure of. And make sure you put into practice all those wine-tasting methods you've learned in the last chapter to get the most out of the experience: serve it, see it, swirl it, smell it, sip it.

SWEETNESS FROM FRUIT:	California Zinfandel
SWEETNESS FROM OAK:	Australian or California Chardonnay
TRULY SWEET:	Late harvest Riesling, such as *Spätlese* or *Auslese*
DRYNESS:	Sauvignon Blanc from France
ACIDITY:	Alsatian or Austrian Riesling
TANNINS:	Young French Cabernet (Bordeaux)

THE WINE SELLER'S DILEMMA

So put yourself on my side of the counter. Sweet, smooth, sour, soft, dry—these are all very general terms that are commonly used, often misused, that describe sensations that could come from a number of different factors. On top of that, everyone has his or her own unique senses of taste, smell, and touch. What is perceived as "sweet" or "smooth" by one person may not evoke the same qualities in the next. So what's a wine merchant, sommelier, or waiter to do?

You will save the day by taking charge of the situation. Soon you'll be well armed with a very specific approach to describing what you like. But when you are talking overall qualities, a little understanding of the elements that make up balance will help. Try to use words like *acidity, tannins, oakiness*, and *fruitiness*. If you're more comfortable sticking to the vocabulary of *dry, smooth, sweet*, and *soft*, come up with a wine, or a grape, as an example of something you think exhibits the particular quality you're seeking. It's to your benefit to give us guys behind the counter *something* to go by. Work with us. We wine guys really do want you to get what you want.

CHAPTER FOUR

WEIGHT TRAINING

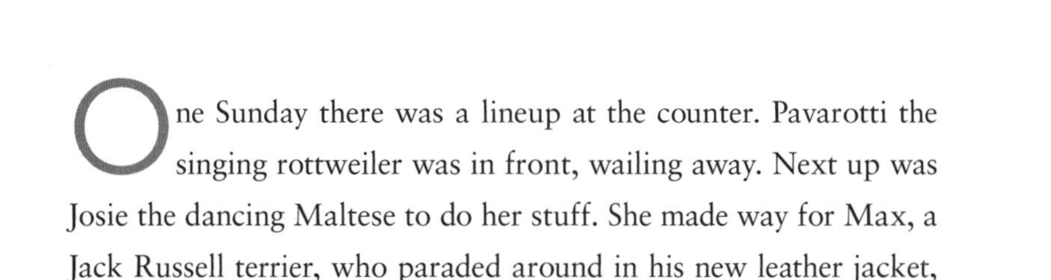

One Sunday there was a lineup at the counter. Pavarotti the singing rottweiler was in front, wailing away. Next up was Josie the dancing Maltese to do her stuff. She made way for Max, a Jack Russell terrier, who paraded around in his new leather jacket, followed by Mr. Jefferson, the standard poodle eager to show off his "roll over and hide" act. Each and every one of them was rewarded with an identical milk bone from behind the counter.

But their human owners needed more individual attention. They weren't all about to walk out of there with the same bottle of wine. They each had specific needs, and to get them what they wanted, we needed to take it one simple step at a time.

The first step, when it comes to finding the wine that will satisfy your specific needs, should be body. Specifying body preference is a huge help to the person who is trying to help you select a bottle. In fact, it is the first consideration that should be made, even before the designation of red or white.

Although body is a major aspect of the overall flavor experience (mixed with balance and taste), it seems to be a hard concept for many of my customers to comprehend. Most people don't think of wine in terms of weight, but it will be easy to understand, once you learn how to taste specifically for that attribute.

When you taste a wine, you can feel its weight in your mouth. The feeling is actually more one of density than of weight. Conceptually, think thick versus thin, both of which are perfectly fine. Think of how you order your coffee—with cream, whole milk, or skim milk. Not only can you see the difference, but you can feel it in your mouth. Thick does not mean gooey or syrupy, but rather producing fuller, richer, bolder sensation, as found in Cabernet Sauvignons and Chardonnays. Thin does not mean watery or weak; light-bodied wines, like Pinot Noirs and Sauvignon Blancs, are lighter, brighter, and airier. Big flavors can be present in any-bodied wine.

WEIGHT CONSCIOUSNESS 

Where a wine sits on the scale is determined by two things.

The primary factor is the grape itself. Grapes can be classified as light-, medium-, or full-bodied. So being familiar with how a grape is generally categorized is the first clue when it comes to body.

The second determining factor is the alcohol content per volume in the wine. Body weight parallels alcohol content—the higher the alcohol content, the more full-bodied the wine; the lower the alcohol, the lighter-bodied the wine. So if you want to figure out how light or full a wine may be, look at the label. You can find this information somewhere on every bottle of wine. All labels are different, so you may have to do some searching. Generally, light-bodied wines range from 7 to 10.5 percent in alcohol content and medium from 10.5 to 13 percent, while the full-bodied big boys weigh in at higher than 13 percent.

Another clue used to determine a wine's body is referred to as "legs." If, after you swirl, the wine slowly runs down the inside of the glass in long streams, then it has legs. Legs, an indicator of high alcohol content, tell you that a wine is full-bodied.

TASTING FOR WEIGHT

It's time to taste some wines and compare them for their body. I suggest that you approach this by doing comparative tastings, using wines from extreme ends of the weight scale. It's the fastest and easiest way to experience the differences.

REDS:	*LIGHT-BODIED:*	Oregon Pinot Noir
	vs.	
	FULL-BODIED:	California or Australian Cabernet Sauvignon
WHITES:	*LIGHT-BODIED:*	Riesling or Pinot Grigio
	vs.	
	FULL-BODIED:	California or Australian Chardonnay

To compare two wines, pour enough for a large mouthful of each into a separate glass. Put the two glasses next to each other. Look at them. What do you see? Good old logic is at work here. In general, the lighter the color, the lighter the body.

Taste the wine that's lighter in color first. Close your eyes and "weigh" it while it's in your mouth.

Eat something bland like a water cracker or a piece of bread between wines, to neutralize your taste buds, cleansing your palate for the next taste. A sip or two of water also helps.

Then do the same with the darker wine. Take note of how it feels in comparison to the lighter one.

If you can't determine which wine is fuller than the other, clear your palate and start over. The worst that can happen is that you *have* to have another sip or two of wine. That would be a shame!

EVERY BODY IS BEAUTIFUL

With any luck you'll find that wines from across the weight spectrum appeal to you, because the really great thing is that you can pick your body type to fit any occasion. The wine world is a wonderful world where a big, fat, full-figured body is often as desirable as a light, delicate one.

Body is a particularly important consideration when you're looking for something to go with food, even before you lock yourself into a choice of red or white. There are big and bold whites, like Chardonnay and Viognier, as well as light, bright reds, like Beaujolais and Pinot Noir. Keeping your color options open allows you a wide variety of choice. But the correct body weight is non-negotiable.

Pairing body with food is a matter of logic. Delicate foods call for lighter, more delicate-bodied wines. Richer, bigger fare necessitates wine that can stand up to it. You don't want your wine to overwhelm your food, nor do you want your food to devour your wine. There are other elements to consider, namely balance and taste, when pairing wine with food, but weight has to be the first stop.

Now, what if you're just sipping, as opposed to pairing your wine with a meal? I hear a lot of "We're just going to have a glass of wine before we go out." Or "We need to bring a before-dinner wine." Here, weight becomes a personal preference, or something that might be determined by other factors. Take weather, for example. Warmer days call for lighter-bodied wines, such as Sauvignon Blanc or Beaujolais. A glass of hearty Syrah will take the edge off a winter chill. If you are planning on eventually following up your sipping with a meal, think about the type of food you'll be having before choosing a "warmup" wine. Pick something that won't conflict with the cuisine. Personally, I prefer a lighter-bodied wine before a meal, no matter what the time of year and no matter what kind of chow is coming up. Wine with a lighter body tends to whet your appetite, rather than overwhelming the meal to come.

ACCEPT THE BODY FOR WHAT IT IS 

When you know the ideal weight you're after, look for a grape that fills the bill. Anyone who requests a "really, really light Cabernet Sauvignon" or a "big, full-bodied Pinot Grigio" is no more likely to succeed than someone seeking a waiflike sumo wrestler. You need to come to terms with the wines' weights. It really starts with the grapes.

Varying degrees of weight can come from a particular grape, depending on the alcohol content of the wine. And there are aberrations out there, like some Pinot Noirs that actually have more alcohol per volume than some Cabernet Sauvignons. But those Cabs will still come off as fuller-bodied than those Pinots.

Grapes must be loved for what they are. You can't expect them to be something they're not. If you want a red on the lighter side, pick a Merlot or a Sangiovese. Leave that poor Cab alone. And don't turn to a Pinot Grigio if you're looking for a big white. Try a juicy Chardonnay, and stop expecting that poor Pinot Grigio to be a powerhouse.

	REDS	WHITES
LIGHT-BODIED	Cabernet Franc Dolcetto Gamay Grenache Pinot Noir	Grüner Veltliner Pinot Gris/Pinot Grigio Riesling
MEDIUM-BODIED	Merlot Pinotage Sangiovese Tempranillo Touriga Nacional	Albariño Chenin Blanc Sauvignon Blanc
FULL-BODIED	Cabernet Sauvignon Malbéc Nebbiolo Syrah/Shiraz Zinfandel	Chardonnay Gewürztraminer Viognier

CHAPTER FIVE

MEET THE GRAPES

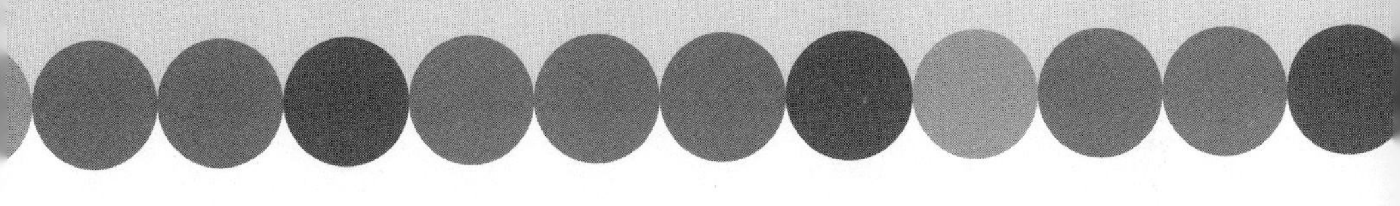

I admit to having a love affair. There's no denying it. The proof is right there on our fridge: photos of me all over the world, surrounded by spectacular scenery, grinning from ear to ear, eyes twinkling with delight, arms amorously embracing . . . the vines. My wife should have known what was coming after spending our honeymoon being dragged from tasting room to tasting room. But who could blame me? After all, it was during one of the best Napa Valley vintages ever.

My infatuation with grapes can be easily explained. It comes from the simple fact that that's where wine begins. Every grape variety has a unique set of characteristics that it brings to the flavor of its wines. So to understand flavor in wine, we need to go straight to the source.

Remember, wine flavor is a combination of taste, smell, and touch. You should have the touch part down by now, in terms of body. That's a great place to start. But it's not enough simply to know that you want, say, a full-bodied red or a medium-bodied white. That leaves the field of choices way too open, and by relying only on body you might end up with a wine you find unappealing.

To narrow it down, you must dig a little deeper into flavor, this time by applying your senses of taste and smell.

Thousands of grape varieties are used in winemaking today. But don't panic; there's no need to get to know them all. For now, you'll be tasting your way though some of the most common varieties. Eventually you'll be able to pick and choose from grapes you may not be at all familiar with, using what you've learned about your own preferences to match flavor characteristics to those grapes that share similar qualities.

I've provided just a few facts about each grape, to arm you with the "need-to-know" info. But the most basic, and most important, thing to learn about them is what flavors they evoke in you. Keep the goal in mind: *to identify and articulate flavor.* That's it. Sound easy? Well, it is and it isn't. Knowing whether or not a wine appeals to you is the easy part. The question you have to ask yourself is *why?* And to answer *why*, you have to be able to identify and articulate *what*. What does the wine taste like?

WALKING THE WALK 

Not everyone has the natural ability to identify individual aromas and tastes that come from a wine. But it's a skill that can be acquired. That's why they call it having an *educated* palate. And just think of the fun you'll have teaching it. You simply need to focus on the task, then let it happen. And the best part is that it gets easier with practice.

Take it slowly. As you work your way through the grapes, try to dig deep down inside yourself for a visceral reaction to what you are tasting. But don't try too hard; let it come to you in its own time. Give your senses, and your brain, a chance to think it through.

Use your imagination. Forget everything you think you know about the flavor of grapes. Let's start from scratch. As you take in that first whiff and that first taste, you must make sure your mind is free of any preconceived thoughts about flavor. Let your nose and mouth use their imaginations. Don't let your brain take over by coming up with words it may have heard used before to describe wine. Allow yourself to free associate. The aromas and flavors you detect may remind you of something you have never connected with wine before, such as bananas, wet rocks, or tobacco.

Trust your instincts. Let your gut lead the way. It's important to remember that, when identifying flavor, there are no right or wrong responses. Although certain aromas and tastes are definitely inherent in vinified grapes, everyone experiences them differently. Have confidence in yourself!

Raise your consciousness. You have learned that your nose has an amazing ability to remember. But what about your brain, and its ability to take those sensory memories to the next step? It's your brain's job to process your reactions and file them away for future use. You must remember to remember.

I don't know how many times I've heard things like, "I had the best wine of my life the other night at a restaurant. But I can't remember what it was. It had a picture of a bird on the label. Do you have it?" And it's unbelievable how many people can come up with only "it was red" or "it began with a C" as a description of a particular wine they're trying to recall. "Stump the Wine Guy" is not a game either of us wants to play. I must admit, I have been known to locate a bottle based on label design, but it's not easy.

Even the best of us, unless we have a photographic—or in this case, taste-o-graphic—memory, may have to use some aids to help remember what we do and don't like. Everyone has his or her own methods of recall, so choose the ones that work best for you. You can save labels, even if you're at a restaurant. You can write on a napkin, or on your hand. Ask your waiter to write the name of a wine you like on the back of a business card. Do whatever it takes to remember a wine that particularly strikes your fancy. Just pay attention. Be conscious of what you are drinking.

Remembering a wine because you are dead-set on replicating an experience is one thing, but you may not be able to find that exact bottle again. Nor is it really crucial that you do. The ability to recall a specific wine you flipped over is most useful as a clue for you and your wine seller, your waiter, or your sommelier, when you're trying to discover *new* experiences you might enjoy. You can point to that bottle you remember as something you like, which may help him or her lead you to similar choices.

But what if a wine seller, waiter, or sommelier isn't familiar with the particular wine you name? Without being able to describe anything else about it, how are you going to be able to leverage that wonderful experience into more wonderful experiences?

Any information is good information when you're attempting to describe a wine that appealed to you, when the goal is to find others that you might like. Remembering a specific wine is a start. Being able to recall a grape is even better, and should actually be easier. Adding information about where the wine came from will certainly help point you in the right direction.

But once you can think and communicate in terms of flavor, a whole world will open up to you. Identifying *why you liked* a wine gives you the most flexibility, and therefore the most potential, when it comes to finding new and exciting treasures.

TALKING THE TALK 

I've never eaten a lead pencil or, for that matter, buried my nose in some good, scrubby underbrush. Yet both those terms are accepted language when it comes to describing certain wines. Granted, many words used to describe wine flavor seem a bit absurd. But because the "experts," such as critics and judges, need to apply standard terms to describe what they detect, these words have become the accepted vocabulary in the wine world.

You, too, will learn to talk the talk, to a point. At least the more practical, obvious descriptors will become part of your lexicon. But not just yet. The more important thing for you to do, at first, is to try to come up with your own language to describe what you are tasting. You may or may not come up with the same words the "experts" use, but for now that doesn't matter. (If you come up with something like "saddle leather" or "corrupted cherries" on your own, then you are a real natural.) Your immediate mission is to train yourself to discern aromas and tastes. You can't handcuff your senses by expecting them to respond in someone else's words.

Remember, if your first impression evokes tactile words like *sour*, *smooth*, or *tangy*, try to detect what qualities might be causing that sensation. Is there a hint of oak? An acidic element that's coming off as sharp? The more specific you are, the more effective your communication skills will be. But above all, be sure to go beyond that first impression and delve into the actual aromas and flavors swirling around inside that glass.

Here's a helpful hint: there are no descriptors unique to the wine world. Wine flavor is described only in terms of other things, most often fruits, sometimes vegetables or even flowers. Obviously, wines aren't made from those things; they're simply reminiscent of them. In fact, it has been proven that wine has a molecular structure similar to all of them. You also may want to think in terms of spices, nuts, herbs, and confections. But don't limit yourself. A wine can evoke all sorts of identifiable flavor characteristics. The question you should be asking yourself as you taste is, "What does it remind *me* of?"

That said, it would be nice if you could just stick forever to your own wine vocabulary. But you should become familiar with the terms most often used to describe wine on back labels, shelf talkers, and wine lists. And using words from the standard terminology will help you communicate better with wine sellers, waiters, sommeliers, and fellow wine lovers. To converse effectively, you will need to speak a common language.

So after, and *only* after, you articulate your own responses to a particular grape, check your description against the words most commonly used to express that grape's flavor. One hopes you'll have some words that match, or at least come close to the common descriptors. If not, taste again. Now do you detect any of those qualities? Even if you did come up with some of the same responses, taste again. Are there perhaps other layers of flavor the experts' words evoke that you didn't uncover the first time around?

Many experts use adjectives that personify a wine, such as *assertive*, *clumsy*, or *awkward*. I've even heard a Burgundy described as being "oafish." Oooookay . . . but it's hard to imagine those words being useful in many situations. Even comparisons to other fruits are sometimes obscure. How many of us really know what lychees or gooseberries taste like? Use the vernacular only when it makes sense to you, when you can actually taste those same characteristics in a grape.

MATTERS OF STYLE

There is not one definitive answer to the question of what a grape tastes like. There are not even two definitive answers. If only it were that simple! You already know one reason for this—every person tastes a little differently. On top of that, a singular grape can evoke a huge spectrum of aromas and flavors, depending on the style of a particular region or winemaker and on the climate in which it was grown. The good news is that this provides plenty of choices, with plenty out there to appeal to each and every one of us. And once you know a little bit about how these factors affect a wine, it's really not difficult to figure out what you can expect in terms of flavor.

OLD VERSUS NEW

Style, generally speaking, can be linked to geography. In the wine world, it largely comes down to a matter of Old World versus New World—France, Germany, Spain, and Italy on the Old side, and the United States, Australia, New Zealand, South America, and South Africa on the New.

In the Old World, winemakers have relied on centuries of grape-growing experience to develop unique styles that reflect the traditions of their regions. In fact, the driving force behind Old World style is the belief that the land itself overrides the winemaker in terms of importance. The grape is supposed to naturally express the land on which it is grown. So strong is this tradition that Old World wines are named after *where* they are from, as opposed to *what* they are from. This is why a Pinot Noir is called a Chambolle-Musigny when it comes from that particular town in Burgundy, or why a Sangiovese is referred to as Chianti when you're buying it from that particular region in Tuscany. In order to be allowed the privilege of using those regional appellations on the label, winemakers must adhere to a series of strict rules that control what can and can't be grown, what can and can't be blended, and what can and can't be done to the grapes during the growing and vinification processes. Old World wines come with a solid guarantee, in terms of flavor.

The New World, not so bound by tradition, has gone about things in a whole other manner. Basically, anything goes. Without all those rules and regulations, and with a general populace that doesn't have many preconceived expectations regarding flavor, the "new kids on the block" have had the freedom to experiment and to stretch the boundaries of what wine can be. They've created a whole new style, one in which the fruit itself is pushed onto center stage. With the unrestricted application of science and technology thrown into the mix (used to manipulate the process and extract as much flavor as possible from the grape), you've got a culture in which it's the winemaker, rather than nature, driving the train.

So how does all this affect flavor? The two approaches result in completely different styles that are fairly obvious to detect. I boil it down to "Less Is More" versus "More Is More." Old World style leans toward the understated and reserved, and New World to the big and brazen. With Old World wines, you can detect a subtle sense of the earth blended with the fruit flavors, sometimes with tastes like mushrooms or minerals, for example. New World wines, on the other hand, shout out, "Fruit, fruit, fruit!"

Then there is the oak factor. While both worlds use oak barrels during the fermentation or aging processes, they use them very differently. In the Old World, oak is used more subtly to slightly enhance flavor. In the New World, for the most part, newer wood is used, and the wine sits in those barrels for longer periods. The result is a more intense color, odor, taste, and feel.

Old World wines are built to last longer than most New World wines—the more natural winemaking style means more tannins and more acidity, which gives the wine a longer life. While they are drinkable when they hit the shelves, they'll probably go from good to extraordinary as time passes. New World wines, with their full fruit flavors, lower acidity, and lower level of tannins, are made to be consumed immediately. They will age, but not for as long a period as Old World wines. However, the quest for immediate gratification seems to be creeping into other cultures, and as a result more and more Old World winemakers are responding by adjusting their techniques accordingly.

Styles are beginning to cross over in other ways as well. In fact, in the Old World, it's now common to encounter some "internationalization" of wines. Europeans are beginning to make wine specifically to appeal to the tastes of Americans and the rest of the lucrative New World market, our tastes having been defined by the typical style of the wines we produce. In some cases, European styles are even being geared to the personal tastes of top New World wine critics. High ratings translate into big bucks (or euros). On the other side, there is a movement by a number of New World winemakers to try to replicate the subtler wine styles of the Old World. For them, it's a matter of seeking a point of differentiation in a crowded, competitive marketplace.

Many in the wine world fear the outcome of this boundary-hopping of styles will be a world in which all wines taste alike. This is doubtful. The crossover is still fairly minimal, the Old World appellation laws are still in place, and no matter what, winemakers will continue to produce a variety of styles, as long as they appeal to consumers.

Two worlds, two styles, and two great alternatives. I say *vive la difference!* You'll probably find your personal set of preferences reflects a mix of both Old World and New World wines. As it should. There is no good or bad, no right or wrong in this case. Each style has its place, depending on your meal, your occasion, or simply your mood.

THE WEATHER FACTOR

The way climate affects style is simply logical. In warmer regions, the sun beats down on those vines all season long. By the time harvest comes, you've got higher sugar levels, which means lusher, juicier, fruitier grapes, and fuller-bodied wines. Cool weather results in leaner, more acidic, subtler fruit, and comparatively lighter-bodied (although not necessarily light) wines. In term of flavors and aromas, those warm-weather grapes tend to evoke tropical sensations (for example, pineapples, mangoes, passionfruit, and melon) in whites, and darker fruit (like plums, figs, and blackberries) in reds. Cooler-weather grapes come across with flavors and aromas like citrus and green apple in whites, and redder fruits (red berries, cherries) in reds. Think of it logically. How does heat affect fruit? Which fruits thrive in hot-weather climates? Which can be grown in cooler regions?

But what if you don't know, say, whether the Loire region of France is considered warm or cool, in terms of grape-growing? Here's a simple rule of thumb: climate can be linked to the Old World/New World division. Climate and tradition overlap to make style. For the most part, Old World wine-growing regions tend to be located in cooler climates. New World wines, in general, come from warmer regions. This is not to say there aren't climate variations within countries, regions, and even within some vineyards themselves, but as a generalization, Old is cold; New is hot.

It's pretty straightforward. Once you know your personal preferences, or determine what you want for a particular meal or occasion, you can use climate and geography as predictors of what bottles will feature those flavors.

TASTINGS

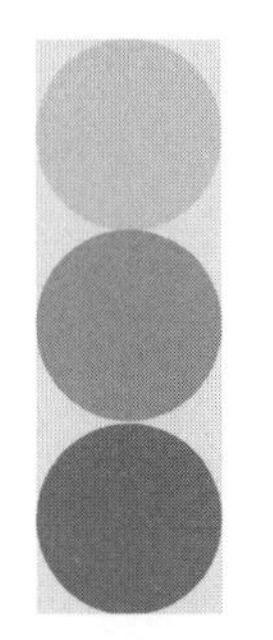

I've chosen eight grape varieties for you to concentrate on. I call them the "Everydays." They represent the most common varieties, grapes that the vast majority of wines all over the world are made from.

Keep in mind that many wines are made from a combination of grapes. Winemakers develop their own blends based on the different qualities each grape brings to the table. After you become familiar with the grapes, you should experiment to see how they work in tandem. But when picking bottles for your tastings, try to find wine made 100 percent from the grape you're tasting. This can get tricky, especially with Old World wines that are named for a region (such as Burgundy, Rioja, or Bordeaux) or producer (such as a winery, chateau, domaine, or bodega) as opposed to a grape. And some wines simply have made-up names! On top of that, many wines that are actually blends list only the predominant grape on the label. The solution? Ask for help if you're not sure. If you need help figuring out what to request when buying the Old World wines, use the charts found at the back of this book.

What you won't see here are suggestions for specific labels. But please don't think I'm trying to make your life difficult. On the contrary: there's no need to waste your time running around looking for something you may not be able to find. Remember those folks who shopped till they dropped? Nor will I direct you to specific vintages. Things change; vintages disappear. Besides, the whole point is to learn to be adventuresome—not for me to be telling you exactly what to drink.

What you need to find is a good representation of each grape.

Although a single type of grape can result in a multitude of wines with extremely different tastes, some universal traits of the variety should be detectable in the final product.

Almost all the tastings can be done with very affordable wines. I've indicated with a dollar sign the few cases where you may have to spend a little more. But for the most part, there's no need to go high-end here. You'll be able to figure out those grapes no matter how much you do or don't spend.

As you make your way through the Everydays, I recommend tasting the varieties individually. This will allow you to focus on each grape's unique characteristics. When there are varying styles that exist for a particular grape, I've suggested you try two wines—one from each end of the style spectrum—so you can experience the full range of flavors and aromas one grape can evoke. Try to taste both styles in one sitting. It's the best way to grasp the signature qualities of each.

If you prefer, you can taste more than one grape at a time. Comparison tastings can be an efficient way to discern differences. If you do choose to go that route, follow the suggested comparisons. I've deliberately chosen grapes that don't share a lot of common characteristics, so the respective flavors will be pretty obvious when one is pitted against the other.

You may want to choose which grape to sample based on a meal you're planning. I've included some "tried and true" pairing suggestions, along with some of my own favorites—ones I often recommend to my customers when they ask for advice. But these are just suggestions. Don't be reluctant to try any pairings you wish. Whatever you do, be sure to taste a little wine before you start eating, when your palate is fresh. Also be sure to pay attention to how that wine evolves over the course of a meal.

While working your way through these tastings, you may find

that one grape appeals to you more than another. Try not to look at this in terms of deeming one "better" than the other. I too often get asked questions such as "Which is better—a Pinot or a Syrah?" That's like asking, "What's better, an apple or an orange?" The question you should be asking yourself at this point is, "What qualities do I detect in this grape, and do they appeal to me?" That's it. End of story.

THE EVERYDAY WHITES 

CHARDONNAY

I sell tons of Chardonnay. In fact, it has been the largest-selling white wine in the United States for years, outselling all other white wines combined. So why is it that I get so many people demanding to be shown anything but Chardonnay? Even some who do buy it often apologize for liking it.

Poor Chardonnay! It really gets a bum rap. I never thought that I would be the one defending it. True, long before I became the Wine Guy, California Chardonnays were practically the only white I drank, but then there was a point when I went cold turkey.

What happened? Like many people who've adopted the "anything but Chardonnay" (a.k.a. ABC) attitude, I got sick of it. And with good reason. The grape is so widely planted, and produces so many wines, it's like someone turned on a Chardonnay spigot. With a volume like that, there are bound to be a good amount of mediocre results.

On top of that, many Chardonnays are indistinguishable from the rest. Most New World winemakers create only the oaky, syrupy, buttery style that comes from an overmanipulation of the grape. They're making what people have become used to, and what many people continue to like. But what can come of this are one-dimensional, flabby fruit bombs with zero acidity and even less character. The manipulation obliterates what little natural acidity the grape has. And this is what turns the ABC crowd off.

But Chardonnay-bashing really isn't fair. The entire category certainly doesn't deserve to suffer. Personally, I've come full circle, and am now proud to show my new respect for this Rodney Dangerfield of whites. The fact is that Chardonnay is the most versatile of white wine grapes. A friend of mine who teaches a wine course likens the Chardonnay grape to a blank artist's canvas. What's created in the bottle can end up being anything from a Dalí to a Degas.

Chardonnays can range from crisp, bright, fresh, minerally, and medium-bodied all the way to lush, rich, supple, and sometimes fat and full-bodied. Those of my customers who paint all Chardonnays as undrinkable, gloppy butterballs are blown away when they try a steely Chablis or an elegant Pouilly-Fuissé. I have to remind them that all white Burgundies are made from the Chardonnay grape. Score one for Chardonnay.

In New World wine regions, many winemakers are starting to back off the oak considerably, in some cases leaving the wood entirely out of the process, turning to steel tanks instead. And it's not just because steel is cheaper to use. These winemakers have torn a page from the success of their Old World counterparts in Burgundy and elsewhere, and are hoping to replicate that success by mimicking the Old World style.

The great thing about Chardonnay is that you can have it any way you like it. So if you're one of those ABC folks out there, give it another chance. Try an Old World Chardonnay you may never have tasted. And if you are someone who loves those big, oaky California or Australian Chardonnays, be proud of it. You're entitled to.

And don't be too shy to share it with others. Chardonnay is a good bet for gift giving, if you're looking to play it safe. Even with all the controversy, it remains very popular. If it doesn't go with your host's meal, it can easily be used as an aperitif. Or your host can save it—it ages well, especially those white Burgundies.

Because Chardonnay is so plentiful, there are tremendous bargains from all over the world, especially the United States, Australia, South America, and certain regions of France, including parts of Burgundy. There's a Chardonnay style and price point for everyone. All you need to know are your style and price parameters, and *voilà*—instant satisfaction.

What to Taste:

OLD WORLD	White Burgundy
NEW WORLD	California or Australian Chardonnay

Compare to:

Sauvignon Blanc

Food Pairings

Chardonnay, with its full body, can go with a wide variety of foods, but it can overwhelm lighter dishes. It's just about the only alternative if you're eating foods more often paired with red but don't feel like having a red.

Grilled sweet corn
Meaty fish (swordfish, tuna)
Pork
Roast or grilled chicken
Salmon
Shellfish
Veal

Aromas and Flavors

Baked bread
Butter
Butterscotch
Chestnut
Cream
Grapefruit
Green apple
Hazelnut
Honey
Honeysuckle
Lemon
Mango
Melon
Mineral
Oak
Peach
Pear
Pineapple
Steel (a.k.a. flint)
Smoke
Sweet corn
Vanilla
White peach
Yellow apple

PINOT GRIS

From my perspective as the guy behind the counter, I can't overlook Pinot Gris. Pinot Gris, especially in its Italian incarnation, Pinot Grigio, is just too popular to ignore. Aside from Chardonnay, there is no white wine that comes close in year-round appeal and sales to Pinot Grigio. It's the comfort-zone wine to millions, and it's easy to understand why.

Pinot Grigios are, for the most part, very light, crisp, easygoing, and pleasant. Add to that the fact that they are usually extremely affordable and widely available, and you have the keys to their success. For these very same reasons, I think Pinot Grigio is a good wine for those who are just getting into drinking wine. I've often suggested it as a starting point for novices looking for a beginner's white. For satisfaction and reasonable quality at a low cost of entry, it's a good choice. Later on I take off the training wheels, but it's a good place to get people up and running.

Pinot Gris *can* get more serious, especially when we're talking about the richer, bolder, honeylike wines from the Alsace region of France. These are definitely more exotic, but also more expensive. And then there's Oregon, which is well known for making excellent Pinot Gris, more in the style of Alsace than of Italy.

If you've never tried a wine made from Pinot Gris in any of its forms, give it a go. And if you have friends who are cautious about getting into wine, bring them a bottle. This one should help them cross the wine-loving threshold.

What to Taste:

OLD WORLD	Italian Pinot Grigio
NEW WORLD	Oregon Pinot Gris

Compare to:

Chardonnay

Food Pairings

Because of its light body, Pinot Grigio is a good accompaniment to lots of light, summery foods.

Light fish dishes
Light pasta
Mild cheeses
Poultry
Salads

Aromas and Flavors

Apricot

Citrus

Green apple

Honey

Lemon

Lychee

Pear

RIESLING

I can hear it now. *Eeew! Don't talk to me about Riesling. They're all too sweet.* That's what I used to get every time I brought up the word. But now I've turned the tide with a bunch of my customers, and they're grateful. I urge you to give my personal favorite white grape a chance, too.

True, Rieslings *can* be very sweet—the ones that are meant for dessert. But the bulk of Rieslings on the market are dry, off-dry, or just slightly sweet, and perform an amazing balancing act. They'll give you tons of fruit up front, and then will reward you with a burst of acidity to temper it. The acidity makes them racy, the fruit makes them spicy, and their light body means low alcohol.

The slight sweetness that some Rieslings exhibit is what makes them go so wonderfully with all kinds of different foods. Try to imagine what a touch of sweetness, combined with razor-sharp acidity, might do for a heavy, fatty, spicy, or creamy dish, for example. We're talking heaven here.

The most famous Rieslings come from their native Germany, where they are subject to a fairly involved classification based on the amount of residual sugar (sweetness) in the wine. In simple terms, the driest classification is *Kabinett*, followed by *Spätlese*, then *Auslese*. Look for these words on the labels. You might want to try each one to get an idea of what they represent. There are other classifications beyond these three, which will take you into some of the finest dessert wines in the world. But the bulk of German Rieslings on the shelf will be *Kabinett*, *Spätlese*, or *Auslese*.

Two other things to note about German Rieslings: as much as they are recognized for their greatness, they are also known to be extraordinary bargains. Sure, there are some extremely pricey German Rieslings, but there are also many outstanding ones available for $20 and under, and they age well. I've sampled forty-year-olds that are just hitting their stride.

World-class Rieslings are also made in the Alsace region of France, as well as in Austria, where they tend to be drier than the ones from Germany. Beyond that, Riesling excels in the cooler climates of California, Washington, and New York, and in New Zealand and Australia. There are bargains galore from all regions. So some night when you're going to sit down to a seriously heavy meal, treat yourself to a Riesling. Not only will it make the meal special, it will also help lighten the load.

What to Taste:

OLD WORLD	German Riesling
NEW WORLD	Australian Riesling

Compare to:

Chardonnay

Food Pairings

Riesling's wide range on the dry-to-sweet scale, coupled with its acidity, give it the ability to work well with all kinds of foods. In my opinion, it's the most versatile white wine to accompany food, bar none. A little bit of sweetness complements a salty or spicy meal, and a little acidity goes a long way in cutting through richness and cream. I am always on a campaign to make Rieslings part of everyone's must-have list.

Chicken
Cream-based sauces (for pasta and other foods)
Fish
Ham
Omelets
Pork
Salads
Shellfish
Spicy Asian cuisine
Turkey
Veal
Vegetarian dishes

Aromas and Flavors

Apple
Apricot
Citrus
Grapefruit
Honey
Honeysuckle
Jasmine
Lemon
Lime
Mineral
Nectarine
Peach

Pear
Rose
Steel (a.k.a. flint)
Tangerine

SAUVIGNON BLANC

Sauvignon Blanc has been on a roll for the past few years. Perhaps part of its success, at least in this country, is a result of the Chardonnay backlash. But I think a lot of it has to do with the fact that the wine is just so darn interesting and tasty.

First of all, there's that unforgettable aroma, one that will make you an instant wine expert at any blind tasting—what many folks uncharitably dub eau de cat piss. There is even a New Zealand wine called Cats Phee on a Gooseberry Bush. But trust me, it *tastes* nothing like that. *Zingy*, *zippy*, *zesty*, *racy*, *refreshing*, and above all *grassy* are adjectives that come to my mind when describing Sauvignon Blanc.

Sauvignon Blancs range from light- to medium-bodied, and can exhibit a wide range of flavors depending upon the climate in which the grapes are grown. They all have plenty of eye-opening acidity. I love them for their versatility, too. They're equally at home at picnics, barbecues, and five-star meals, where that crisp acidity acts as a natural palate cleanser. On their own (not blended with other grapes), they're not really built to last, so enjoy them within a year or two of bottling.

This grape is grown all over the world. All by itself it makes two of the great white wines of the Loire Valley in France—Sancerre and Pouilly-Fumé. When it's combined with the Semillon grape, you get the gorgeous, underrated, and unusually long-lived white Bordeaux wines of Graves and Pessac-Leognan, as well as the world-famous dessert wines of Sauternes. In Northern California and

Washington, where it's also known as Fumé Blanc, Sauvignon Blanc is second only to Chardonnay in white wine popularity. It has propelled New Zealand into becoming a world-famous winemaking region in just a matter of a decade or so, is the backbone of the white wine industry in South Africa, and is on the rise in South America and Australia as well.

Styles vary greatly. You'll find more subtle and restrained qualities in Sauvignon Blancs from the cool Loire region, for example, than you will in those from warmer California. And the extremely long growing season in New Zealand, with its long periods of sunshine, produces an even more pungent style, with tropical flavors in the grape. It's best to eventually sample something from each of those three regions (where most of the Sauvignon Blancs you'll see are from) to find the one that best suits your palate. From my experience, Sauvignon Blanc lovers are very specific, set on the style they like best and rarely deviate from it.

Like Chardonnay, Sauvignon Blanc is plentiful, and that translates into extremely affordable. Give it a whirl.

What to Taste:

OLD WORLD	Loire Valley Sauvignon Blanc (Sancerre, Pouilly-Fumé, Quincy, or Touraine)
NEW WORLD	California or New Zealand Sauvignon Blanc

Compare to:

Chardonnay

Food Pairings

Sauvignon Blanc's acidity works great for cutting through fried or creamy dishes. Its body also makes it a good match for lighter cuisine. It's a nice aperitif as well!

Chicken
Fresh cheeses (goat and feta)
Mild/delicate fish dishes
Oysters
Salads
Sushi
Vegetarian dishes

Aromas and Flavors
Asparagus
Citrus
Cut Grass
Gooseberry
Grapefruit
Green apple
Herbs
Lemon
Lemongrass
Lime
Melon
Passionfruit
Steel (a.k.a. flint)

THE EVERYDAY REDS

CABERNET SAUVIGNON

If you're hearing strains of "Hail to the Chief" in the background, you're right. It's King Cab. The Chairman of the Board. *Capo di Tutti Capi.* You get the idea. The Cabernet Sauvignon grape makes some of the most sought-after wines in the world, and is considered by many to be the noblest of reds. Oddly enough, it's the offspring of a red *and* a white—Cabernet Franc and Sauvignon Blanc. Hence the name.

Cabernet Sauvignons are big, strong, full-bodied wines with plenty of tannins. This characteristic can make them seem austere when they're young, but the tannins are an important factor in the aging process. And believe me, these wines age very well. Aging in oak does a lot to mitigate the astringency, as does blending Cabernet Sauvignon with other grapes. Blending also helps make the wine more complex, because each grape used in the blend brings something to the table.

In Bordeaux you won't find a wine made from 100 percent Cabernet Sauvignon. There it acts as the team captain for most wines made in the Graves and Médoc regions (which include the appellations of St-Estèphe, Margaux, St-Julien, Pauillac, and many other lesser-known appellations). In these regions, it's blended with Merlot, Cabernet Franc, Petit Verdot, and Malbéc in varying combinations to make the wine that best pleases each individual winemaker.

On the other side of the world, Northern California often produces 100 percent Cabernet Sauvignons, many of which are recognized and sought after by wine lovers everywhere. The warm California climate produces less tannic fruit, thus making the wine less austere and more immediately user-friendly. But over the past few decades blending has been on the rise in California, and it is now a common practice. There's even a relatively new category of California wine called Meritage (rhymes with heritage), which is made with at least two of those Bordeaux grapes. By law these wines can be made only in limited amounts, and must be made from only the highest quality of grapes of the chosen varieties.

Cabernet Sauvignon is grown in every winemaking country in the world. It loves warm climates and is a staple in Australia, Chile, Argentina, Italy, and South Africa. Because it's so prevalent and relatively easy to grow, there are many excellent values. Most wines made from Cab will be a blend, but there are plenty of "straight" Cabs available, too. Look for bargains from South America, Australia, and California in particular. There are also lots of bargains from Bordeaux, especially from some of the lesser-known appellations. But wherever your Cabernet comes from, you'll understand instantly what this nobility thing is all about.

What to Taste

OLD WORLD	Red Bordeaux $ (St-Estèphe, Margaux, St.-Julien, Pauillac, Graves, Médoc, Haut-Médoc)
NEW WORLD	Australian or California Cabernet

Compare to:

Pinot Noir

Food Pairings

Cab's invariably rich and full-bodied nature demands that it be paired with a meal that can stand up to it.

Beef
Game
Hearty stews
Lamb
Semi-firm cheeses
Strong, smelly cheeses

Aromas and Flavors

Anise
Blackberry

Black cherry
Black currant
Black olive
Black tea
Cassis
Cedar
Cherry
Chocolate
Eucalyptus
Green bell pepper
Licorice
Mint
Plum
Raspberry
Tobacco
Tomato
Vanilla
Wood

MERLOT

The royal red bloodline continues with Merlot—another noble red. Unlike Cabernet Sauvignon, Merlot has achieved unbelievable heights with regard to its popularity and worldwide success. Why? Because of its nature. If Cabernet Sauvignon is the tough, demanding iron-fisted ruler, Merlot is the gentler, more reasonable second-in-command. It's like the guy who calms down his hot-headed friend before a fight can break out.

Merlot is easygoing, soft, round, and juicy. Its medium build and lack of austerity (which comes from relatively low levels of tannins and acidity) make it very approachable, likeable, and satisfying—ergo popular. It's the essence of the "smooth" that is so often cited by my customers as a desirable red wine characteristic. And this is what has made Merlot the success that it is today.

But lately Merlot has suffered a bit of the same fate as Chardonnay. Mass plantings in every wine region around the world have led to a lot of mediocre, uninteresting wines that have brought a "sameness" to the market, and with it a slight trend away from Merlot.

Though there are many stunning 100-percent Merlots out there (such as Château Pétrus from Bordeaux and many others from Northern California), Merlot's real strength lies in its ability to blend beautifully. Wines that are a bit more complex and interesting result when Merlot is teamed up with other grapes.

This is not a bulletin to Bordeaux winemakers. They've been casting Merlot as the main player, with Cabernet Sauvignon and Cabernet Franc assuming supporting roles, for almost three centuries, with fabulous results. If you've never tried a St-Emilion or a Pomerol, you owe it to yourself to someday do so. The Italians blend Merlot with Cabernet Sauvignon to make many of their coveted "Super Tuscans." Yum. And don't forget those pricey Meritages from California—Merlot is one of those Bordeaux grapes that can be found in the blend.

The practice of blending Merlot is taking hold almost everywhere. Chances are good that the California Merlot you see on the shelf today is going to contain some Cab Sauvignon or Cab Franc, or both. Merlot is used as a blending grape in lots of the wonderful reds from Washington and South America. The only winemaking region that is an exception is Australia, where Merlot plantings are limited and Shiraz (a.k.a. Syrah) assumes Merlot's role as the blending grape of choice.

While there are many high-end Merlots in the world, bargains galore exist from just about anywhere, as the grapes are easy to grow and are planted everywhere. So Merlot is a super every-dayer whether it's from the United States, South America, South Africa, or some regions in France. It is still the "go-to" safe red to bring to dinner if you're not sure of what's being served, thanks to its ability to please almost everyone.

If you're already a fan of Merlot, continue to enjoy it. If you're one of those who thinks they may have had enough, give it another try—this time in a blend.

What to Taste:

OLD WORLD	Red Bordeaux **$** (St-Emilion or Pomerol)
NEW WORLD	California or Chilean Merlot

Compare to:

Syrah

Food Pairings

Merlot works well with medium to heavier cuisines. Its relative softness makes it a fine partner to acidic, tomato-based dishes as well as a full range of meats and cheeses.

Burgers
Duck
Grilled meats
Meaty fish (tuna, swordfish)
Pizza
Pork
Prime rib
Red pasta sauces
Semi-firm cheeses
Veal

Aromas and Flavors

Anise
Black cherry
Black currant
Black olive
Blueberry
Boysenberry
Cedar
Cherry
Earth
Eucalyptus
Fennel
Green bell pepper
Green olive
Licorice
Mint
Plum
Raspberry
Red currant
Spice
Strawberry
Tea
Tobacco
Vanilla
Violet

PINOT NOIR

It's hard for me to be objective about this grape. I'll confess right now—Pinot Noir happens to be my favorite red. That's not to say that I don't love all red wines. But this one, when done to perfection, is truly special. *Sensuality* is the one word that comes to my mind when describing the perfect Pinot Noir.

But when not done right, yuck! And it is easy to screw up a Pinot Noir. The grape is an extremely difficult one to cultivate, and the degree of failure is high. It's thin-skinned, temperamental, unreliable, inconsistent, and a genetic nightmare. And there isn't a winemaker out there who wouldn't love to conquer it.

Because of its thin skin, Pinot Noir needs a cooler climate than a Cabernet Sauvignon or a Merlot, which leads to a lighter-bodied wine. The warmer the climate, the fuller the body. But Pinot is never grown in *too* warm a climate, so it's rarely full-bodied. What you will get from that cooler-climate grape is wine that's silky and soft, with low tannins but high acidity. And a wine that can age and evolve for decades.

When you buy a Pinot, you'll get a full-fledged Pinot. The grape is rarely blended with other grapes. It's been said that no other grape takes on the characteristics of the climate, soil, and growing conditions of a specific region more than Pinot Noir. That's why you'll find the wines to taste completely different from region to region, country to country.

Pinot Noir is *the* red grape of Burgundy, where the wines represent the Holy Grail to Pinot growers, winemakers, and drinkers alike. In addition to the Burgundies, most of the Pinot Noirs you'll see on the shelves will be from California, Oregon and, more recently, New Zealand. While Oregon and New Zealand Pinots resemble Burgundy's in style, because of their similar climates, California is in a world of its own. The California heat brings out a fruitiness and fullness in the grape that you won't find anywhere else.

Everyone asks why Pinot Noirs are so expensive. The answer is simple: high maintenance and low yields lead to high cost. There are a *few* deals to be found. I've come across some tasty bargains from California and Oregon, and even a couple from regions in France outside Burgundy. But buyer beware. With a really low-priced Pinot, you'll probably get what you paid for. So even if you have to stretch your wine budget a bit, go for it. Both you and the wines are worth it.

What to Taste:

OLD WORLD	Red Burgundy **$**
NEW WORLD	California Pinot Noir

Compare to:

Cabernet Sauvignon

Food Pairings

Pinot is one of, if not *the,* best food wines—a wonderful accompaniment to lots of different foods, thanks to its relatively high acidity level and its juicy, rather than thick, texture. It loves food, and food loves it. Just about anything goes, though the wine is really not full-bodied enough to put up against "big" food, such as heavy grilled meats like lamb or steak.

Creamed soups
Duck
Grilled or smoked salmon
Meaty fish (tuna and swordfish)
Pork
Roast/grilled chicken
Smoked cheeses
Soft ripened cheeses
Veal
Vegetarian dishes

Aromas and Flavors

Bacon
Black cherry
Black plum
Black truffle
Cherry
Chocolate
Clove
Cranberry
Raspberry
Rose
Smoke
Strawberry

Vanilla
Violet
Wet earth

SYRAH (A.K.A. SHIRAZ)

You say po-tay-to, I say po-tah-to; you say Syrah, I say Shiraz . . . Whichever you call it, they're the same grape. The Australians and South Africans are the ones who call it Shiraz, harking way back to its possible Persian origins. To add to the confusion, some California and Argentine winemakers are starting to call it Shiraz as well.

Whatever it's called, Syrah's popularity has boomed over the last couple of years, making it the Merlot of the New Millennium. Everybody is getting in on the act: plantings have increased by 5,000 percent worldwide over the last ten years, with Australia leading the charge and California, Washington, Italy, Spain, South Africa, and South America not far behind. It's reached the point where I'm seeing a few new Syrahs/Shirazes pop up every single week. And it's a good thing that there's plenty to go around. This formerly little-known grape from the Rhône region of France has become the everyday darling of wine lovers around the world.

The most famous Syrahs come from the Northern Rhône region, with names like Hermitage, Crozes-Hermitage, Côte-Rôtie, Cornas, and St-Joseph. They're all 100 percent Syrah, with the exception of Côte-Rôtie, where the winemakers might throw in a little Viognier to brighten the wine up a touch. These are serious, earthy, rich reds with a serious price tag to match—and a favorite among serious collectors.

In the Southern Rhône, Syrah is a critical component of Châteauneuf-du-Pape, Côtes du Rhônes, Gigondas, and Vacqueyras. Since the grape is blended with others, these wines aren't as massive or chewy as their northern cousins. And the Languedoc region of France is gaining a new respectability for its wines thanks to the introduction of Syrah into its blends. What were once thought of as eminently forgettable cheap red table wines have now become deliciously memorable, thanks to Syrah.

But it's the New World, and Australia in particular, that's behind the recent meteoric rise in this grape's popularity. The hot climate of the Southern Hemisphere makes it a Shiraz playground. These wines definitely have their own style—less earthy and much fruitier than that of their French counterparts. Friendly Australian Shirazes have taken the marketplace by storm, at friendly prices—in many cases well below $10 a bottle. And while there are many delicious inexpensive ones available, there are just as many world-class Australian Shirazes being made and exported at world-class prices.

In the United States, California and Washington have become the primary sources of excellent Syrahs. Initially the competition from Australia was a challenge in terms of cost and marketing, but now that U.S. plantings have increased there are plenty of good values on the shelves. Syrah does particularly well in South Africa and South America, where it is readily available at any price point.

Wherever it is, this is a grape that loves a hot climate, and it reacts to the heat by getting riper and richer, as opposed to sweeter. Its wines are full-bodied, spicy, even peppery, and extremely ageworthy. And they're lip-smacking good.

What to Taste

OLD WORLD	Northern Rhône Red **$** (Hermitage, Cornas, Crozes-Hermitage, Côte-Rotie, or St-Joseph) or other French Syrahs (find one that has the grape listed on the label)
NEW WORLD	Australian or South African Shiraz

Compare to:
Merlot

Food Pairings

Syrahs are not for the faint of heart—you need big food to wrestle these guys to the ground. These are wines that can make your August barbecue a success, but can also warm you on a raw, nasty day in February.

Barbecued/Grilled foods (even salmon and chicken)
Duck
Game
Lamb
"Meaty" veggie dishes (like ratatouille)
Pork
Spicy ethnic foods (Indian, Turkish)
Steak
Stews
Strong cheeses

Aromas and Flavors

Black currant
Black olive
Black pepper
Black truffle
Blackberry
Cherry
Chocolate
Cinnamon
Clove
Eucalyptus
Plum
Raspberry
Red currant
Rosemary
Sage
Smoke
Spice
Tar
Thyme
Vanilla

Fig
Leather
Licorice
Mint
Wet earth
White pepper

CHAPTER SIX

THE BREAKAWAYS

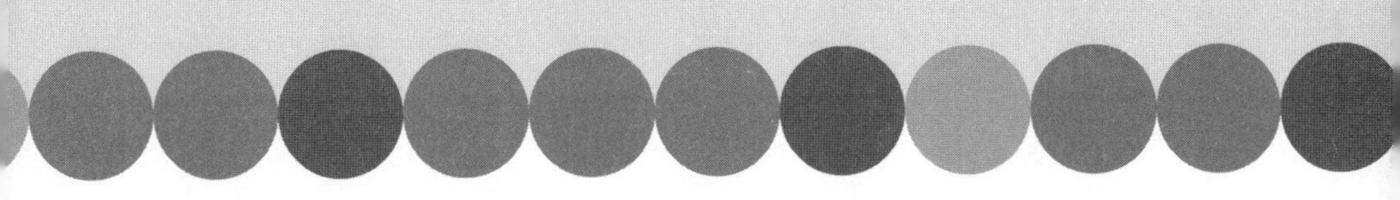

One of the best things about being the Wine Guy is getting the accolades. *What a beautiful store. Wow—you have a terrific selection! Love your handwritten descriptions of the wines.* I've actually been credited, believe it or not, for bringing "joy and happiness" to New York's Upper West Side. Wow!

But what really makes me feel good is getting positive feedback from customers I've steered beyond the usual suspects to the next tier, to grapes they may never have experienced before. When I hear things like *Thank you for teaching me to love Grüner Veltliner* and *Where has Tempranillo been all my life?*, I know I'm doing something right.

Now that you've become very familiar with the Everydays, you can use what you've learned about your personal preferences to venture into what might be unknown territory. These "breakaway" grapes are ones that aren't usually top of mind, either with the wine buyer or the wine seller, yet they all make exciting, interesting, and delicious wines. I think of them as my hidden treasures, the ones I move toward when I sense that a customer is ready and willing to explore a little further. Many represent good values, are good choices for either everyday or special occasions, and go great with food. Some will be easy to find, but for others you may need to dig a little deeper. Grab them when you see them, and give them a shot.

THE BREAKAWAY WHITES 

ALBARIÑO

This superb white grape comes from northwestern Spain (Galicia), where the locals' diet consists of fish, fish, and then some more fish. It's also planted widely in Portugal, where it's called Alvarinho. Albariño makes beautiful, rich, exotic white wines perfect for any seafood imaginable. I've made a lot of friends with this one—it's amazingly refreshing, unique, and delicious, like biting into a crisp, green apple that has a drop of honey on it to counterbalance the tartness. If you can find one, try it. It will make you smile.

CHENIN BLANC

The best expressions of this grape are the white wines from the Loire Valley. You'll find them on the shelves with names like Vouvray, Chinon, Saumur, Anjou, Savennières, and Montlouis. The grape is so versatile that it can be vinified dry, semi-dry, sweet, and sparkling, and exhibits wonderful flavors reminiscent of ripe red apples and peaches. The sweet Chenin Blancs are some of the most sought-after dessert wines in the world, and they age for decades. Look for appellations like Quarts de Chaumes and Coteaux du Layon for a dessert wine experience beyond your wildest imagination.

Wines from this grape are also widely available from South Africa, where it's also known as Steen. While they're not as dramatic and memorable as the wines from the Loire, they are extremely gulpable (pleasurable, nice and refreshing) and affordable. Take a Chenin to a summer picnic sometime. It will reward you with a lovely wine/food experience.

GEWÜRZTRAMINER

I think the only thing holding back the success of this grape is the thought of having to ask for it by name. It is tough to pronounce, yet easy to love.

Gewürztraminer is very distinctive in sight, aroma, and taste. The wine's deep gold or peach color comes from the fact that the grape is actually pink. When you take a whiff, your nose will be treated to an explosive, flowery aroma that's almost pungent, setting you up for the taste. *Gewürz* in German means "spice," so take that as a hint.

Even though these wines thrive in cool climates, they're unusually high in alcohol. This makes for a big, opulent white, with a floral spiciness that's unmistakable. Gewürztraminers can be dry, off-dry, and sweet (if they are "late harvest"), but never bone-dry. There will always be a touch of sweetness, but that's what makes them perfect for highly seasoned, salty, and spicy foods, especially Asian cuisine. Gewürztraminer's full body can stand up to rich foods, and in its sweetest form it's great with fruit or as a dessert wine. These wines should be enjoyed young, certainly within two years of the vintage.

The most famous Gewürztraminers are made in the Alsace region of France, on the border of Germany. Alsatian late-harvest wines are known throughout the world. The grape also does well in the cooler climates of Germany, Austria, Italy, New Zealand, and the Pacific Northwest. Bargains can be found from Alsace and

Washington State, but in general, Gewürztraminers are a little pricey.

GRÜNER VELTLINER

If you find this wine in your local store or restaurant, treat yourself. Grüner Veltliner is an Austrian white grape that goes with just about everything. Take it on a picnic, or roast a chicken, or grill a fish and wash it down with a "gruvee," and you're in heaven. The wines are medium- to full-bodied, dry, pale, crisp, and most important, spicy, a quality that really gives them that something special. They have excellent acidity, which, combined with their full body, makes them one of the most versatile food wines in the world. They can even work with some of the most challenging food pairings around, such as asparagus and artichokes. Now, that's versatile!

While most Austrians drink them young, Grüner Veltliners age very well. You can find these wines at a wide range of price points, from the extremely affordable (about $10 to $15) to the very pricey (well over $30). There's no reason to go to the high end to find out how good they are. I haven't disappointed a single customer with this wine recommendation.

VIOGNIER

I've turned many of my customers on to Viognier, and they've flipped over it. I'm thrilled when they return and ask for it by name, as if they've been drinking it all their lives.

Viognier is my first suggestion for those who want to take a break from Chardonnay, yet still want that full-bodied white wine experience. The wines are definitely reminiscent of Chardonnay, with their low acidity and big, rich fruit. But Viogniers are just different enough—more floral, with unique fruit flavors—to make them a distinct alternative. Like Chardonnay, Viognier will stand up to rich, full cuisines. Treat it like a red if you must, though personally I wouldn't have it with a steak.

Viognier originated in the Rhône Valley, where the fabulous white wines called Condrieu are made. It is also used in small amounts to add vivacity to the outstanding red Côte-Rôties. And if you've ever had a white Côtes du Rhône, you've experienced Viognier as part of the blend, along with two other white Rhône Valley grapes, Marsanne and Rousanne.

Now Viognier is making a name for itself as a stand alone white in Northern California, Australia, and the Languedoc region of France. The California versions are expensive because they're limited, but there are values to be found from both Australia and France.

THE BREAKAWAY REDS

CABERNET FRANC

Here's another grape that I'll get on a soapbox for. Whenever I drink Cabernet Francs, I find them to be utterly enjoyable, without being flashy or brassy. They're just plain good. The fruit is soft, earthy, and luscious, with a very distinct herbal aroma and taste that make the wine compatible with many foods. I often recommend putting a slight chill on them. When customers come in looking for a light- to medium-bodied red that's not overly bright and fruity but complex enough to go with just about anything, I inevitably steer them in the direction of a Cabernet Franc.

Cabernet Franc is one of the primary blending grapes of Bordeaux, along with Cabernet Sauvignon and Merlot. But rarely will you experience it in a dominant role, with the exception being one completely unaffordable Bordeaux—Cheval Blanc.

In the Loire Valley, Cabernet Franc is the primary stand alone red grape, and the wines are just fantastic. Chinon, Anjou, Saumur, and Bourgueil are all made from Cabernet Franc. They're reasonably priced, and are the purest example of what this grape is meant to express.

This is another cool-climate grape, which can make bigger, bolder wines when exposed to a lot of heat. It's now widely planted in California, Washington, New York, New Zealand, and Northern Italy. Most often it stands alone, but it is sometimes blended, as in the Meritages of California.

For some, Cabernet Franc is an acquired taste, so don't give up on it if you find the first couple of sips strange. Hang in there and you'll be rewarded.

DOLCETTO

A beauty from the Piedmont region of Italy, this grape makes reds that are really bright and fruity, with fresh red berry flavors that are best enjoyed young. These are not wines for the ages. If the vintage is over two years old, pass.

Dolcetto means "little sweet one," and despite their high acidity, the wines do taste slightly sweet. I think of them as the Italian Beaujolais because of their eminent gulpability, and I'll steer a customer who likes a good Beaujolais to a Dolcetto for a similar, yet unique, experience. The wines go great with mushroom-based pasta dishes, tangy veal or pork, as well as spicy Asian dishes with curry or other hot condiments. As with a Cabernet Franc, you may want to throw a little chill on them.

You'll recognize these wines when you see labels like Dolcetto d'Alba or Dolcetto d'Asti, which means that they're Dolcettos from those particular areas of the Piedmont. Dolcettos are definitely affordable, most coming in at under $20. You will certainly have fun with them, so take one home some night.

GAMAY

If you've ever had a Beaujolais (named after the wine-growing region south of Burgundy), you've experienced the Gamay grape. But if you're one of those people who balks at Beaujolais because of the Nouveau thing, then hold it right there.

Not all Beaujolais are Beaujolais Nouveau. Beaujolais Nouveau is a once-a-year phenomenon, when, on the third Thursday of November, tens of thousands of cases of new Beaujolais, harvested, fermented, and bottled within a window of weeks, get rushed to wine shops and restaurants around the world. It's a symbol of the holiday season, it's fun, and it's affordable. I sell a ton of it.

"Real" Beaujolais comes in three types—simple Beaujolais (coming from any undesignated area in the region), Beaujolais-Villages (from one of thirty-nine villages, sometimes named after the village), and *cru* Beaujolais (named after the top ten villages in the region—no "Beaujolais" on the label). All these wines are more substantial than Nouveau, yet still bright, fruity, juicy, versatile, and enjoyable. They're low in alcohol and high in acidity, which makes them a great accompaniment to lots of foods. Don't let the Nouveau prejudice stop you from trying one of those *crus*—like a Morgon, a Fleurie, a Moulin à Vent, a Julienas, or a Brouilly. The last appellation is probably the most recognizable. I've heard "I didn't know Brouilly is a Beaujolais" more than once.

These are wines meant to be enjoyed young, slightly chilled, and with light foods. What could be better on a hot summer day on a picnic or at a barbecue? They're fun and affordable, so chill one and chill.

GRENACHE

Characterized by low acidity, high alcohol, and a certain amount of spiciness, Grenache makes excellent, extremely affordable red wines that are great as aperitifs, or when paired with many lighter foods. Its fruity, bright red berry flavor, along with its light to medium body, puts it somewhere between a Gamay and a Merlot. You're usually going to find this grape blended with lots of others in wines such as Châteauneuf-du-Pape, Côtes du Rhône, Gigondas, and Vacqueyras from the Southern Rhône region in France. It's blended with Tempranillo in Riojas from Spain, where the grape is known as Garnacha, and in wines from California.

But Grenache is standing on its own more and more, especially in Spain, Australia, and the Languedoc region of southwestern France. As with Dolcetto, enjoy the 100-percenters young, as they have a tendency to oxidize within a year or two. Give these wines a whirl. They're real crowd pleasers!

MALBÉC

For centuries, Malbéc has been an important blending grape for the wines from the Bordeaux and the Loire Valley regions, and the grape that makes the "inky, black" wines of Cahors, also in France. The wines made from Malbéc in France are highly tannic, earthy, and dark and can sometimes taste pretty nasty if the grape is not blended with a softer one like Merlot.

The hotter climates of South America, particularly Argentina (where it's the most widely planted red grape), have tamed Malbéc, producing wines that are highly accessible and delicious. The Malbécs of Argentina are rich and deep, with plenty of alcohol and juicy, dark ripe fruit, but with much softer tannins than their French cousins.

Wines made from Malbéc are perfect when you're in the mood for a thick, juicy steak or a cozy, hearty stew. Because the grape is so widely planted, there's plenty of it. And because there's plenty of it, the wines are extremely affordable, starting at less than $10. So go out, buy yourself a bottle and some red meat, and have a ball.

NEBBIOLO

I pride myself on finding great wines at reasonable prices. But sometimes a grape makes wines that are truly great, yet never reasonably priced. Does Barolo or Barbaresco ring a bell? These are two of the "splurge" Piedmontese reds made from Nebbiolo, and they're worth springing for.

These wines are characteristically bold and aggressive, and they practically invented the word *robust*. High in acidity and tannins, they can be stored for decades. Look for the oldest ones you can find. As they age, they mellow without losing any of their powerful qualities.

Black fruit, tar, and leather are all typical descriptors of the wines from the Nebbiolo grape. There are lighter Nebbiolos from other regions in the Piedmont, such as Ghemme and Gattinara, which might remind you of a voluptuous red Burgundy. But no matter what part of the Piedmont they're from, these wines have enormous character and complexity.

There isn't a food that Nebbiolo can't tackle, and the richer the better. Stews, ragouts, red meat—bring 'em on. And while I don't usually recommend decanting, these are wines that definitely thrive with a little breathing room. So pick an occasion, break open the piggy bank, and treat yourself to the noblest of Italian grapes.

PINOTAGE

I call Pinotage a love/hate wine, because customers who try it either bring it back and ask for something else or put me on their holiday card list. Fortunately, most of them have really enjoyed it, and now buy it regularly.

Pinotage is a hybrid grape made from crossing Pinot Noir with a fairly ordinary French red grape called Cinsault. The result is a grape that makes wines I've dubbed "Pinot Noir on steroids."

These wines are usually light-to-medium-bodied, but can also be big, full, Zinfandel-like reds, with lots of rich black raspberry and currant flavors. They all have a definite chalkiness or dustiness, which is the quality that will make or break the wines for you. Pinotages are not at all expensive, and are a versatile food wine. You may have to hunt around a bit for this one, but if you're one of the many who find it appealing, you'll be rewarded for your efforts.

SANGIOVESE

Chianti, anyone? Sangiovese is the principal grape of central Italy, which includes Tuscany—the home of the Chianti region. When I was a kid, Chianti was a cheap, crummy red wine sold in a bottle wrapped with a wicker basket (appropriately called a fiasco). What a difference a few decades make. Today that Sangiovese grape is making wonderful Chiantis, as well as other amazing wines from all over Italy, including the majestic Brunellos di Montalcino.

The wines made from this grape are relatively high in acidity, and you'll find a wide range of body types. It all depends on where the wine is from, and on the quality of the grape. The wines range from medium-bodied for the young, basic Chiantis to medium- and full-bodied for the long-lasting Chianti Classicos, Brunellos, and Rossos of Montalcino. The fruit is rarely overwhelming, which makes the wines versatile enough to go with many different foods. I like them with just about anything Italian, as well as with barbecued food and hearty winter meals.

Sangiovese blends well with a number of other red grapes, including Cabernet Sauvignon, Merlot, and Syrah. These blends create "Super Tuscans"—now some of the most coveted wines from Italy. Not much of the grape has been planted outside of Italy, and what has, hasn't resulted in very good wine, including the Sangioveses from Northern California.

Bargains exist with simple Chiantis, Sangioveses, and Sangiovese blends from Tuscany, as well as from other regions like Emilio-Romagna, the Marches, and Umbria, where the wines will be made of some, if not all, Sangiovese.

TEMPRANILLO

If there's a better value in the wine world than Spanish wines, I don't know it. The Spanish section of West Side Wine is one of my favorite spots, because the price-to-quality ratio is so ridiculous. And Tempranillo is the grape that's making it happen, with the wines from Rioja and Ribera del Duero.

Like the wines of the Sangiovese grape, Tempranillo-based wines are medium- to full-bodied, with high acidity and earthy, dark fruit. Similarly, they can be drunk young yet age pretty well, and are a great partner to many foods. I think of Mediterranean cuisine when I think of Tempranillo. The reds of Iberia are made for spicy, flavorful, rich, hearty fare.

The grape shines even brighter when teamed up (like Sangiovese) with others, such as Cabernet Sauvignon and Syrah, to make much more complex, expensive, age-worthy wines. In fact I do recommend, without hesitation, a Tempranillo-based wine to anyone who wants a change from Sangiovese, and vice versa. I promise that the experience will be equally rewarding.

Spanish wines are the ultimate "bang for your buck" values of the Old World, as are those from Portugal, where Tinta Roriz is the name for Tempranillo. Prices are beginning to creep up, but plenty of steals are still available and will be for some time to come. Run, don't walk, to the Spanish section next time you're in the mood for a bottle of red that will completely satisfy you at a price that will make you want to buy two.

TOURIGA NACIONAL

I love the wines from Portugal, and this red grape is probably the best of the bunch. It makes dark, earthy, tannic wines filled with lots of rich plum and black currant. The wines are rarely huge. The rich fruit, in conjunction with generous acidity, makes them enjoyable with light to medium dishes, including fish. I like these wines slightly chilled. They're another welcome guest at a picnic or barbecue. And to top it all off, theses wines are cheap! How about $6 for an aperitif or a delightful dinner companion? You'll be hard pressed to beat it.

ZINFANDEL

Kaboom! That's the sound of a Zinfandel as it hits your mouth. That's not a bad thing, by any means, but you should be prepared for the experience.

To say that these wines are full-bodied is like saying Einstein was good in math. I once tasted a showcase Zinfandel at a high-end California winery and pegged its alcohol level to be 16 percent tops. I was blown away when I found out it was *over* 18 percent! That's a little extreme, but it gives you an idea of what kind of power these wines can obtain.

In addition to the extraordinary alcohol levels, the wines are uniquely spicy, fruity, and tannic, which allows them to age well, though not as well as a Cabernet Sauvignon. If Zins are muscle cars, then Cabs are luxury cars: the Zin gets out of the gate a lot quicker, but runs out of gas much sooner, and the luxury car will outlast it every time.

Zinfandels have been dubbed "America's Wine." That's because the grape has no significant presence anywhere else in the world, with the exception of the Apulia region of Italy, where Primitivo is grown. Testing has proved Primitivo to be a close, if not exact, match for Zinfandel. The wines from this grape are also quite rich, but no match for the American version. Because it's the only grape we can call our own, Zin has developed a huge loyal following in the United States. There's even a sizable nonprofit organization called ZAP (Zinfandel Advocates & Producers), dedicated to the advancement of knowledge and appreciation of Zinfandels. Just imagine how much fun their meetings must be!

Zinfandels are priced for all pocketbooks, from $9 casuals to $50 cult collectibles. And don't confuse them with White Zinfandel—a sweet rosé made from the Zinfandel grape.

A monster red calls for a monster meal, so enjoy Zinfandel with big food, like you would a Syrah or a Cabernet Sauvignon. These are wines for food, not for lounging. They're a blast, literally.

LET THE EVERYDAYS LEAD THE WAY 

This chart, matching the Everydays to the Breakaways (taking body, flavors, and aromas into consideration), should make things *really* easy for you.

WHITES

If you like this ▶ You might also like this ▼	CHARDONNAY	PINOT GRIS	RIESLING	SAUVIGNON BLANC
Albariño		●		●
Chenin Blanc	●			●
Gewürztraminer	●		●	
Grüner Veltliner		●	●	
Viognier	●			

REDS

If you like this ▶ You might also like this ▼	CABERNET SAUVIGNON	MERLOT	PINOT NOIR	SYRAH
Cabernet Franc	●	●		
Dolcetto			●	
Gamay			●	
Grenache			●	
Malbéc	●			●
Nebbiolo	●		●	●
Pinotage	●		●	●
Sangiovese		●		
Tempranillo		●		
Touriga Nacional		●		
Zinfandel	●			●

FLAVOR FINDERS

You can also let your flavor preferences lead you to new grape discoveries. These charts indicate some of the most common aromas and taste descriptors of the Everydays and the Breakaways.

WHITES

	ALBARIÑO	CHARDONNAY	CHENIN BLANC	GEWÜRZTRAMINER	GRÜNER VELTLINER	PINOT GRIS	RIESLING	SAUVIGNON BLANC	VIOGNIER
Apricot					●	●	●		●
Butter		●							
Citrus	●		●		●	●	●	●	
Coconut									●
Cream		●							
Floral	●			●	●				●
Grapefruit		●					●	●	
Grass			●					●	
Green apple	●	●	●		●	●	●	●	
Herbs			●					●	
Honey	●	●				●	●		●
Honeysuckle	●	●					●		
Lemon	●	●				●	●	●	
Lime								●	
Mango		●	●	●					●
Melon		●						●	●
Minerals	●	●					●		
Nuts		●							
Oak		●							
Peach	●	●	●	●	●		●		●
Pear	●	●		●		●	●		●
Pineapple		●							●
Red Apple			●						
Smoke		●							
Spicy			●		●				
Steel	●	●					●	●	
Vanilla		●							

REDS

	CABERNET FRANC	CABERNET SAUVIGNON	DOLCETTO	GAMAY	GRENACHE	MALBÉC	MERLOT	NEBBIOLO	PINOT NOIR	PINOTAGE	SANGIOVESE	SYRAH/SHIRAZ	TEMPRANILLO	TOURIGA NACIONAL	ZINFANDEL
Anise		●				●	●				●				
Bacon									●						
Banana			●												
Bell Pepper	●	●					●								
Black Cherry		●				●	●	●	●						●
Black Currant	●	●				●	●			●				●	●
Black Olive		●							●			●			
Black Truffle								●	●			●			
Blackberry	●	●			●	●		●				●	●		●
Blueberry							●			●					
Cassis		●						●							●
Cedar	●	●						●							
Cherry	●	●	●	●	●		●		●	●	●	●	●	●	
Chocolate		●				●		●	●			●	●	●	●
Earth					●		●		●	●	●	●	●		
Eucalyptus		●				●	●					●			
Herbs	●											●	●	●	
Leather						●		●				●	●		
Mint	●	●				●	●					●			
Pepper					●	●						●			
Plum	●	●			●	●	●		●	●	●	●	●	●	●
Rasberry	●	●	●	●	●		●		●	●	●	●	●	●	●
Red Currant							●					●			
Smoke									●			●			
Spice					●		●					●	●	●	●
Strawberry			●	●			●		●		●		●		
Tobacco	●	●					●	●			●		●	●	
Tomato		●													●
Vanilla		●				●			●			●	●		
Violet	●		●	●			●	●	●	●					

CHAPTER SEVEN

FINDING YOUR OWN WINE GUY

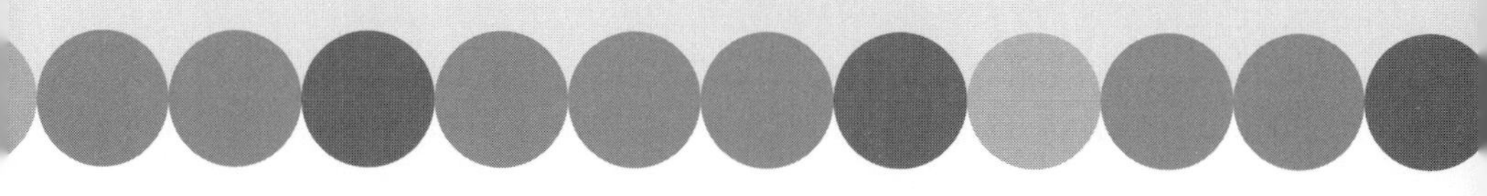

There's a lot of responsibility that comes with being the Wine Guy. The same thing goes for the chicken man in my neighborhood, Mr. Shower Door out in the suburbs, and the Waffle Lady in California. If one type of product is all you sell, your customers have every right to expect you to be knowledgeable about it. *My dinner party is in your hands. You've just got to help me make a good impression on my boss. It's my wedding—it has to be perfect.* Talk about pressure! It's enough to drive a wine guy nuts.

But I applaud those high expectations. Where you choose to shop can be critical to the success of your wine experience. The wine seller's role is to be your support system, your resource, in essence your *partner*. And what have we all been told about that? Don't settle. Visualize the ideal relationship: one with good communication, a high level of comfort, yet full of surprises. You want someone who is reliable yet interesting, someone who has a unique personality and plenty of confidence, and someone who cares about you. It must be someone you feel secure with—someone you can trust.

So how do you find the perfect match? You determine what's

available, and then you go cruising to check out the possibilities. All wine sellers are not the same. Some are better than others. But being better does not mean offering higher-end product, nor does it necessarily mean having the lowest prices. Being better is the result of a number of factors, and above all can only be determined by *your* personal needs and priorities.

As you assess your options, the general criteria should be price, selection, service, and convenience.

Price: Price is certainly important, but it shouldn't always be the overriding factor. Wine prices often vary from retailer to retailer, but usually not wildly. Price is usually determined by volume (the amount the seller buys from the distributor) and by relatively fixed gross margins, which are determined by the retailer. Some wines are positioned as loss leaders to keep the seller competitive, while others (usually ones that are hard to find or not available in large quantities) are priced at a higher margin. Go comparison shopping, and don't buy wine from a retailer whose prices are higher than the competition across the board.

Selection: Bigger isn't necessarily better when it comes to selection. Quality and variety are what count most. However, to be truly adventuresome you'll need to make sure there's a sufficient wilderness of wine to explore.

Service: Service is probably the most variable factor when it comes to buying wine. It can swing from a level of absolutely none, where you might be silently directed to a corner of the store when you say you're looking for an Italian red, to a hovering presence, which can certainly be annoying. Service can be the key to your success, so you'll need to find a venue with a level that you're comfortable with.

Convenience: Shopping for wine shouldn't be a chore, so you should choose a place that fits into your daily routine. But in some cases the perfect partner may not be the most geographically desirable, so you might have to go a bit out of your way to find a good match.

All these criteria are all interconnected. You may pay more for service or convenience in some places, or have to go out of your way for a better selection. In my opinion, your top two priorities should be Service and Selection, with a capital S. However, you may have your own priorities, based on your own particular lifestyle. If you're on a strict budget, price may play a more important role. Or if you have only enough time in your busy schedule to make one shopping stop, the convenience factor might make supermarket wine your best option. And you may not even want to be monogamous—one type of partner may be more suitable for a certain occasion than another.

CHOOSING A PARTNER IN WINE: HOW TO FIND YOUR TYPE

Wine-buying options vary across the country, for the most part dictated by a set of archaic state-by-state laws, many of which are holdovers from Prohibition days. In New York, wine cannot be sold anywhere other than in an actual wine or liquor store. California shoppers can pick up a bottle at any local drugstore. There's a florist in Hawaii who sells wine with his flowers—very convenient for the perfect date. In Michigan, upscale shoppers can pick up a bottle of Barolo to go with their designer jeans at Neiman Marcus. Down in Florida, there's a twenty-four-hour Citgo station with a two-hundred-case high-end cellar and tastings five evenings a week.

There are a few things you should know about all the retail

wine options, at least the most common ones, just so you are aware of how and why they sell the way they do, and when they may or may not suit your particular purposes. In terms of really putting your knowledge to work, some are better options than others. However, since you may not have access to all these types of venues, you should know about how to make the most out of any situation.

Neighborhood Wine Shops. A neighborhood wine shop, if you're lucky enough to have one, could be the ideal match for you (if I do say so myself). If you find a good one, you'll have a partner for life. This doesn't mean you can't stray, but it does mean that you'll have a place to rely on for continuing experimentation and discovery.

Prices at your local wine shop may be slightly higher than at other types of stores, because you will pay more for service, and smaller establishments don't have the advantage of bulk buying. In the long run, though, you may end up actually spending less by partnering with a full-service merchant who knows how to find good values. If your wine seller, say, has a knack for picking out a great, little-known South African Chenin Blanc that costs only $8, you're already better off than you would be buying the big-brand California Chardonnay for $12 at the supermarket.

Just because there's a wine store in your neighborhood doesn't necessarily mean it's a true "neighborhood" shop. Make sure you know what their core business is. Do they specialize in catering to individuals, or are they more of a "front" for a larger corporate, catalog, Internet, or auction business? Some businesses are capable of filling more than one role successfully, so give them at least a shot at satisfying your needs.

Your neighborhood wine shop should carry a variety of bottles spanning all price points. Some stores, particularly in suburban areas, put their emphasis on the high end as a way to compete with supermarket sales.

Be wary of wine stores that call themselves "purveyors." That high-minded name could mean high-brow snobbism and high-end prices. And what's up with sellers of "fine wine"? It's like a restaurant offering "fine food." Shouldn't that go without saying? And really, shouldn't it be better than just fine?

Supermarkets. About 65 percent of the states in the United States allow supermarket sales of wine. The quality of the selection can vary widely, depending on who is doing the buying for the chain. Some California supermarkets, for example, boast a much more interesting selection than wine "specialty" shops elsewhere. Some supermarket chains, and stores that sell specialty food and wine along with other merchandise, often offer interesting private labels or unusual values, but most supermarkets tend to offer name brands. They stick to what is most familiar to the majority of shoppers, so their selection can be somewhat limited.

The humongous volume bought by supermarket chains does give them leverage to buy at great discounts, so they have the ability to sell wine cheaply. Not all supermarkets go that route, though, knowing you will probably be willing to pay more for the convenience factor. And face it, buying wine at a supermarket is convenient. You're already shopping for your food—why make an extra stop for the wine?

As far as service goes, supermarkets can vary. A few have wine experts on hand, and some display detailed shelf talkers to guide you, but that is not the case in most locations.

For those times when you're in a hurry, not in an experimental mood, and know what you want and that they carry it, buying wine at the supermarket fits the bill. If your lifestyle is such that the supermarket is your only wine-shopping option, use what you've learned to make the most of the experience. Find something you haven't tried before. Explore a new region. You'll find some nice surprises.

Warehouse Clubs and "Big-Box" Stores. So you're cruising the aisles with one of those Humvee-size carts, adrenaline pumping from the thrill of all those savings you're racking up. Such deals! Even when it comes to wine. Just be prepared to know what you want, because chances are you won't be able to get much personal assistance. The trade-off for lack of service is usually price and convenience, which do have their merits.

Selection at these types of venues varies. Costco, for example, has made a huge effort to beef up their wine section, and the result has been their current ranking as the largest wine retailer in the country. Their selection is supervised by their own in-house expert wine director, and although they offer mainly domestic wines (lots of brand names) and their inventory isn't vast, they feature a better wine selection than most supermarkets. There are some good deals to be found at Costco, and their selection does include some high-end brands. But, unfortunately, that one wine director can't clone himself to be at all Costco locations to help you. You'll have to rely on their shelf talkers with ratings and flavor guides for direction.

At other stores, such as Wal-Mart and BJ's Wholesale, it's mostly about savings, though some have started to step up their variety and their service. Racks of higher-end wines have been installed in Sam's Clubs, which benefit from having the buying power of Wal-Mart behind them. Target, in its SuperTarget locations, conveniently organizes its wines by color, body, oakiness, and fruit flavor.

Large discount retailers, along with supermarkets, account for nearly 40 percent of all wine sales in the United States. Are you a part of that statistic? If so, take advantage of the discount experience to save some bucks. If there's a wine you know you like, pick up a case. When you want to buy in quantity, for a party, perhaps, think of buying there. No matter what, compare prices elsewhere so you are equipped to recognize a good deal when you see one. Don't assume everything is a bargain. And, of course, always do some experimentation. Read the signage, look at the backs of the bottles for descriptions, and put your knowledge to work.

Wine and Liquor Discount Chains. Though perhaps not as convenient as supermarkets or large discount retailers, wine and liquor discount chains are good options. Since wine and liquor are the singular focus of their business, these types of stores usually offer a wide selection, as well as some level of help. On top of that, prices should be good because of the buying power of multiple locations. Some individual outlets partner with others to form buying cooperatives, and when they do, the savings should be passed on to you.

But you'll have to check out the outlets available to you to see how they match up. If you detect a satisfactory level of service and selection at one of these places, it just may be worth the extra stop.

State-Controlled Stores. If you live in one of the nineteen control jurisdictions, let's hope you live near the state line. You know the situation. Prices are high, selection is limited, and though the staff may be friendly, their hands are tied. They are only allowed to sell what has been preselected by a state board. If you're traveling the country, here's the list:

Alabama	Ohio
Idaho	Oregon
Iowa	Pennsylvania
Maine	Utah
Montgomery County, MD	Vermont
Michigan	Virginia
Mississippi	Washington
Montana	West Virginia
New Hampshire	Wyoming
North Carolina	

Many wine buyers in these states opt to flee, at least when it's time to shop. If this is your fate, take a cue from those folks from Pennsylvania who arrive at my store in New York in droves, empty trunks ready to be filled. But be discreet, because this is illegal.

Direct Sales. Direct sales is a general term used for buying directly from the winemaker or winery by getting on a mailing list, making a virtual visit via the Web, or visiting in person.

A personal visit is by far the most fun and the best option for learning about a winemaker's products. It's a great way to experiment, but unfortunately, more often than not, many of the wines you taste may be allocated. This means there's not enough to go around, and that particular wine may not even make it to your state. In fact, some wines can *only* be found in the tasting room, but don't let that stop you. Take advantage of the opportunity to ask questions, talk to winemakers, and learn how their wine is made.

Many people think they're getting bargains when they buy by the bottle or the case at a winery. Beware! This is the winemaker's one chance to sell at retail, and most of them are going to do it. However, some wineries are starting to discount, usually when they need to move inventory to make room for a new vintage. If you are familiar enough with prices, then go for it.

One more word of caution. There are some legal restrictions that may come into play when purchasing directly from a winery. Although recent legislation has loosened the rules a bit, many states still ban direct shipment of wine. Seven states actually consider it a felony. Some states have reciprocity with others, while others don't. Some limit the amount of wine a consumer can receive, and some require the recipient to have a permit. So if you're hoping to buy a case and have it shipped home, ask first if it can be done. Some wineries are willing to find ways around the rules.

Internet. If you don't like to travel, or prefer to shop with your pants off, then shopping on the Internet may be for you. There are a number of different types of sites that sell wine. Many large retail stores have accompanying sites, where you can buy directly from their inventory and have the order delivered to your door, either directly by the retailer if you're in the area or shipped if you're not. The other type, Internet-only sellers, rely 100 percent on shipping.

Beware that, because this is another form of direct sales, you may come up against the same restrictions that apply to wineries in some states. There is really no consistency in how Web merchants handle the situation, so check the sites' shipping policies before you start to shop. Some get around the rules by having licensed wholesalers ship for them. Others simply state that they take no legal responsibility, and put the onus on you. Also beware that when your wine does arrive, it may be a little battered and bruised, perhaps having been at the mercy of wild weather and even wilder package handlers. Wine needs to be handled with care, so try out different sites to see how well they pack and ship.

Overall, although the bigger retail sites feature the full inventory of their brick-and-mortar stores, the larger online-only vendors tend to have limited selections, focusing mainly on high-volume producers. You should be able to find the same stuff elsewhere. However, with restrictions on direct shipping easing up, things are starting to change. Some small producers are starting to go online themselves, offering wines that are not widely distributed at retail.

And as far as service goes? Even though some sites include "educational" content and descriptions of their offerings on their sites, you still really need to know what you want. Options often include searches by color, region, type, and price.

For the most part, online shopping isn't going to save you a lot of money. Once shipping and handling costs are added in, you're paying about the same as you would in a "real" store. So it's best to focus on those things you can't find elsewhere.

All in all, Internet wine shopping is great for the convenience of long-distance gift giving, and more and more for access to wines you can't get locally. Just know what you want, and don't expect it in time for tonight's dinner.

Auctions. If you truly get carried away by all this wine stuff, you might find yourself someday bidding for rare bottles or interesting lots in an online or live wine auction. There are plenty of auction sites to choose from online, where you can search for specific bottles or browse through the catalog. Live wine auctions, sometimes hosted by large retailers, are often listed in newspapers and wine magazines, as well as online.

There are some steals to be found at auction, especially if you really know what you're doing. If you're into wine as an investment (and have the willpower not to drink it!) or are simply turned on by the excitement of "winning," then good luck to you.

THE TEST—ARE THEY WORTHY? 

Once you have narrowed down your potential wine partners to the ones you think might offer the best service and selection, you're ready for a little cloak-and-dagger work. But first, pay attention to what you can learn about a place before you even walk through the door. Think of it as a blind date. If you don't like what you see, you can just walk away, no hard feelings. To be fair, you should know what you are looking for. It comes down to part vibe, part common sense.

THIS MAY NOT BE THE ONE FOR YOU IF . . .

You can't see through the windows of the store.

If a window is plastered with sales stickers, promotional posters, banners, or neon signs featuring brand names, sound the alarm. This is not the type of place that will go the extra mile to introduce you to little-known, special wines. Those generic cardboard displays are also something to look out for. "Done" windows may mean a "done" deal with a distributor, which means that a place is buying in volume from a particular vendor, and therefore may not have the most diverse selection.

We spent an entire afternoon reliving holidays past when we took over West Side Wine. The faded cardboard Santas had been watching over the neighborhood from the side windows for years. Layers and layers of corrugated decorations had to go. Chimney bricks were covering Thanksgiving foliage, which was covering Stars and Stripes, which were covering the Easter Bunny. After removing about a thousand staples we got out the black paint, and we never allowed a distributor near those window displays again.

The entire window is filled with one brand of wine.

This is another sure sign of a deal made with a distributor. You can be sure that the management here is not inspired enough to feature their own faves. One retailer we knew was notorious for being "bought." His window featured only one very well-known brand, and he even had pictures of the winemaker, by whom he was often wined and dined, all over his store. If you see a particular label over-represented across all lines and varieties, it's a sign of either lazy buying habits or behind-the-scenes deals.

The windows are full of dusty bottles.

One word: lazy. Are they just as lazy when it comes to keeping the inventory fresh and interesting?

There's lots of liquor on display.

You want wine, right? Would you call this place a liquor store, or a wine store that carries liquor?

Once you've found the place that gives off the right first impression, it's time to dig a little deeper. Go inside. Take a good look around. Ask yourself the following questions:

1. How's the air in there?

Coolness, in this case, is a good thing. If a place feels hot inside, the wine is cooking in the bottles—not a good thing. Direct sunlight and high heat are wine's public enemies numbers one and two. Number three is fluctuation in temperature. Chances are if the store is hot one day, it will be cold when the weather changes. The rule? Keep it dark, keep it cool, keep it constant.

2. *Can I find my way around?*

Can you figure out the logic of the store's layout without too much difficulty? Though there are exceptions, most stores are organized by country or region, including mine. Even though I recommend learning grape by grape, it's pretty difficult to display wines that way. Think of the nightmare blends would cause!

Make sure you're not going to waste a lot of time trying to find what you want. If you're confused, it doesn't necessarily mean that the management doesn't know what they're doing, but then again, they should be doing everything possible to make it easy for you. When in doubt, do not hesitate to ask how the store is organized. If they have trouble explaining their system, hightail it out of there.

3. *Is there anything to read?*

Is there signage describing the inventory? If so, does it give you hints about flavor? Does it seem to reflect the owner or manager's personal opinions, or does it look like a sales pitch provided by a distributor or winemaker?

Not all mass-produced signage should be discounted. Often you'll find a description of what the winemaker hopes to express with the wine. That can be useful information. Note that some stores post ratings (Robert Parker's, *Wine Spectator*'s) as a service to their customers. That's okay, but keep in mind that it means the store is using someone else to do their job for them, and that ratings can be overused. Ratings should not substitute for personal opinions. Remember that these ratings are the opinions of only a couple of people, and should not be taken as the Holy Grail. One man's 93 is another's 85.

When you are lucky enough to find a place with personalized shelf talkers that include flavors in their descriptions, try to see if you speak the same language. Test your perceived flavors against theirs. If a wine suggests raspberries to them, it should ideally do the same for you. Not all of your words will match, but you should have enough confidence to be able to use their descriptions as a guide.

4. Do they cover the spectrum?

How many regions are represented in the selection? At the very least, you should find wines from France, California, Australia, Italy, Spain, and South America. Ideally, the selection should also include New Zealand, Portugal, Germany, and South Africa. And if you live somewhere with local vineyards, you should be able to find homegrown bottles as well.

5. How broad is the price range?

Today there are great wines to be found at all price levels, so it makes sense for a store to offer a range of options to its customers. There should be wines for all budgets—from $6 to $100-plus per bottle. Most important, there should be a broad selection concentrating on the $10-to-$20 range, as that's where most of the best values can be found.

One of my customers told me of an experience with a retailer who tried to sell him a $60 Bordeaux as a bulk party wine! When the customer balked and commented that other neighborhood shops would have tons of other, more affordable party wines to recommend, the retailer scoffed and replied, "Well, we don't have those kinds of customers." Well, now they don't have that guy either.

6. What's being pushed?

Take note of any special displays in the store. Ideally they should feature special values or interesting finds, not overstock or hard-to-sell odds and ends. I've found that anything we feature in a basket sells like hot cakes, and I'm sure other wine sellers have witnessed the same phenomenon. Ask why particular wines are being featured. After you've gone back a few times, see if the displays have changed. A good store will be on their toes to keep their relationship with you fresh and exciting.

7. Do they have the goods?

Determining quality at first blush is a difficult task in any situation. It's somewhat subjective, especially with wine, but if a place doesn't carry your favorite wine, that doesn't mean they don't have a good selection. There are thousands and thousands of wines for retailers to choose from.

When assessing quality of inventory, a few adages apply. First of all, bigger isn't necessarily better. Just because one store has more bottles doesn't mean what they've got is good. And don't let the sheer number of bottles fool you. Variety is the spice of life. How many *different* wines are on the shelves? Look carefully.

When I took over West Side Wine, I actually decreased the existing shelf space, which is usually regarded as an absolute blunder in the traditional retail world, but it made sense to me. I wasn't attempting to limit my customers' choices. On the contrary, I was expanding the variety, yet controlling the quantity of bottles displayed. There was no need to visually overwhelm people.

8. Are there any deals?

Is this place offering good values? Are they passing any special savings on to you? It's a hard thing to determine, because all retailers buy differently. They don't all get the same deals on the same products. But if you have the inclination and energy, you can always do some comparison shopping to make sure you're not being ripped off.

9. But what if I see . . .

As you look around, don't rush to judgment. Some of those things we've all been led to believe about wine are no longer the case.

First of all, it's okay if all bottles are not horizontal. It is true that wine, in general, should be stored on its side. Otherwise, corks can dry out and allow air to seep in, which can ruin the wine. But that doesn't mean that *all* bottles need to be on their sides. Some fly off the shelf so quickly that there's no time for the wine to become oxidized. And with the growing popularity of alternative bottle-stoppers, upright storage is becoming less of an issue.

Don't go running for the door if you see large bottles on display, either. No need to think "jug wine." Container size does not determine quality. Would you balk at a magnum of fine Champagne? Many good-quality wines are now available in large formats (in fact, it seems that some even drink better when bottled this way). Today the trend is toward liters, which hold about one-third more wine per bottle than the "regular" size. Liters are a great alternative for those who don't want to commit to a magnum (two bottles in one), yet are still interested in getting more for their money. Larger bottles should offer better values, as you're not paying for "extra" packaging.

Now it's time to get personal. The physical attraction is there, but what about personality and intelligence? What should you expect from the ideal partner? Try this simple exercise.

1. When you walk through the door, you hear
   a. nothing.
   b. someone snoring.
   c. "Hello, can I be of any assistance?"

A greeting is nice. The wine seller should be happy to see you, especially since you're the one with money in your pocket. An offer of assistance is important. And it doesn't mean the seller thinks you look helpless or bewildered. It's just the right thing to do. With any luck, he won't cross that fine line between being helpful and tailing you as if you were just waiting for the opportunity to slip a bottle in your cargo pants.

2. You say, "Yes, I'd like some help. I'm looking for a red wine." He says,
   a. *"They're over there."*
   b. *"Here, try this."*
   c. *"To go with a meal? If so, what are you eating? Or is it just for sipping?"*

These may not be the seller's exact first questions, but question-asking is a good indication that he's making an effort to narrow down your options by listening to your needs. And that's good. The full lineup of questions ideally should cover body, flavor, and price range. If, in fact, you do get this line of questioning right off the bat, you may have made your match.

3. You pick up a bottle. You ask if the seller has tasted it. He says,
   a. *"No."*
   b. *"Me? Never. I'm a Scotch man myself."*
   c. *"Yes, we taste everything we sell here."*

Perhaps it's a little unrealistic to expect a wine seller to have tasted every single thing he sells, but he pretty damn well better have sampled most of it. Vendors offer wine sellers the opportunity to taste before they commit to buying. It's a tough job, but somebody's gotta do it.

4. You hold that bottle up and ask the seller to tell you something about it. He says,
   a. *"It's really good."*
   b. *"It's $12.99."*
   c. *"It's 100-percent Sangiovese from Tuscany. If you've ever had a Chianti, that's the grape it's made from, so it's medium-bodied, similar in weight to a Merlot, with a rich red berry flavor. It goes great with all kinds of food—from pasta with red sauce to a roasted chicken. It's the best we've found for the price. We love this wine."*

Even if he hasn't personally tasted the wine, the person selling it should be well versed in its qualities. At the very least, he should be able to easily tell you what grape it's made from, which, if you have done your homework, should be enough for you to go by.

5. You pick up a really cheap bottle off the shelf. You ask the wine seller what he thinks of it. He says,
   a. *"It's a good cooking wine."*
   b. *"Yuck!"*
   c. *"For the price, it's quite good."*

Even the cheapest wines your wine seller offers should be the best they can be for the price. All wines he stocks should be considered "good," or a good value.

6. You say, "I had an Argentine Malbéc the other night. Do you have anything similar?" He says,

a. *"Never heard of it."*
b. *"No."*
c. *"You might like a Cahors from southwestern France. They're made primarily from Malbéc grapes, too."*

As you now know, every wine can be linked to another by virtue of grape, weight, and flavors. If you have something in mind that you like, there's no need to ever walk out empty-handed.

7. You say you're going to a friend's house for a dinner party and you want to bring some wine. The seller asks you how much you want to spend. You say between $15 and $20. He
   a. *grabs a nearby bottle for $19.99.*
   b. *asks you if you might be willing to spend a little more.*
   c. *shows you a wine that's only $12.99, but that goes great with the duck you said your friend is serving (when, of course, you were asked what your friend would be serving).*

You've gotta love a place that's going to give you exactly what you need, and on top of that not have you spend every penny of your budget. This is a place that is looking to build a business and keep you coming back for more.

8. You go back to the same place a few times. The seller
   a. *acts as if he never laid eyes on you before.*
   b. *asks if you want "the usual."*
   c. *asks if you enjoyed what he helped you pick out the last time, and suggests something else you might also like.*

Again, this shows a desire to build a relationship with you as a loyal customer. And you want the *unusual*, something new and interesting, chosen with care and thoughtfulness.

9. On a return visit, you say you can't remember the name of the wine you bought last time, but you really liked it. The seller
   a. *shrugs his shoulders and says, "Oh. That's too bad."*
   b. *shrugs his shoulders and says, "You should have saved the label."*
   c. *remembers what you bought, looks it up in the computer for you, or tries to help you remember by asking you what you* do *remember about it (grape, origin, flavor, label, etc.).*

Not every wine seller has a sophisticated computer system or a photographic memory, but chances are with a little probing and a walk around the store, a good one will help you come up with the answer.

10. You say you're having a party, and need some help figuring how much wine you'll need to purchase. The seller says,
    a. *"Party! What time? I get off at 10:00."*
    b. *"Figure two to three bottles a person."*
    c. *"It depends. What type of a party is it? Are you serving liquor or beer as well? How many people? And do you think all your guests will be drinking alcohol?"*

This question is a good test of integrity. Does this person have your best interest in mind, or is he just trying to make as much money off you as possible? A wine seller should work with you and tailor the answer to your specific needs, because if you are happy, you'll stay in this relationship for the long haul.

BUT ARE YOU COMPATIBLE?

You get the picture. With a little probing, you should be able to feel confident that you have found a place that offers good assistance, stands by their product, and is smart enough to care about customer satisfaction. Above all, you should feel confident that this is the kind of place you can trust in terms of integrity and knowledge.

The final issue is one of compatibility, and that is something that can be judged only through trial and error. Once you've established that this is the type of place that isn't going to push you to buy something they simply want to get rid of, or sucker you into spending more than you have to, the question is, are your tastes compatible? I don't necessarily mean in terms of *always* sharing the same taste, although that would be nice, but at least you should know they have a good buying sense, in your opinion. How else will you feel secure enough to take a chance on those unknowns they've selected to carry? If you try a wine they've suggested and don't like it, be sure to tell them why, using the words you've learned and the knowledge you've gained. This will help them become familiar with your particular tastes, so they can fine-tune their future recommendations. Give it a few shots. Have a little patience. Sometimes it takes a few dates before you really get to know someone.

MANAGING THE RELATIONSHIP

So say you've weeded through your options and have chosen your wine guy after rigorous scrutiny, based on his performance under fire. That's great. But you can't just sit back and wait for him to ply you with all sorts of wonderful wines that are perfect for you. It takes two to tango. What can you, as the customer, bring to the table to make sure you get the most out of the relationship?

You need to meet your wine seller at least halfway. And you should know by now what that takes: good communication. You now possess the skills to identify and articulate your preferences and needs. Use them!

A mindful shopper is not reluctant to ask for help. He or she doesn't wait to be offered help, but rather demands it. In fact, if I had my way . . .

MY IDEAL CUSTOMER

CUSTOMER: *Good morning. How are you?* (She cares about me!)

ME: *Just dandy.* (Although I've never actually said that.)

CUSTOMER: *Can you give me some help?* (Music to my ears.)

ME: *It would be my pleasure. What are you looking for?*

CUSTOMER: *First of all, I need something to go with swordfish. I usually prefer something full-bodied and slightly acidic, with hints of melon, pear, or honey. I'm* *not a big fan of California Chardonnays, for the most part, although I'm willing to take a chance if you have something you think will work particularly well with this meal. I'm hoping to spend no more than around $15 per bottle.*

ME: *In that case, I would recommend either a Viognier or a white Burgundy.*

CUSTOMER: *Can you tell me how those two compare?* (A great question to use to get a sense of a wine.)

ME: *Well, the white Burgundy is made from Chardonnay, so you'll get more of a pear-apple-lemon kind of thing, and the Viognier will come across as more melon-honey-citrus flavored. Either one will work great.*

CUSTOMER: *Okay. I'll take a chance with the Viognier. I've never tried it before. Sounds good.*

ME: *Way to go! You'll love it.*

CUSTOMER: *It's a big party. I'll need a case.*

ME: *No problem.*

CUSTOMER: (picking up a bottle of Rioja from the shelf) *What grapes are in this one?* (The basic question—and I love her for not thinking she should necessarily know the answer.)

ME: *That's 100 percent Tempranillo.*

CUSTOMER: *I'm not really familiar . . .*

ME: *It's a Spanish grape, similar to Merlot in body, and Sangiovese or Chianti in flavor.*

CUSTOMER: *Sounds interesting. I'll give it a shot.* (Yes! An adventurous soul!)

ME: *Anything else today?*

CUSTOMER: *You sold me a knockout Sancerre the other day. And an amazing white Bordeaux. Do you remember?*

ME: *Of course.*

CUSTOMER: *Knowing what I like, what else would you recommend?*

ME: *How about a Pouilly-Fumé, or a white Meritage from California?*

CUSTOMER: *Okay. I'll try one of each, and I'll let you know what I think.* (Love getting feedback!)

CUSTOMER: *What's your favorite wine right now?* (Great question.)

ME: *Red or white?*

CUSTOMER: *Both.*

ME: *I just got in a terrific Dolcetto from the Piedmont region of Italy. I had it last night with a roast chicken. Superb. And this Albariño is a killer.*

CUSTOMER: *Sold. Give me a case of each.*

ME: *Anything else?*

CUSTOMER: *That will do it for this morning. I may see you again later in the day, though.*

ME: *Okay. I hope you enjoy everything. Let me know.*

CUSTOMER: *You have never steered me wrong.* (Gotta love that blind trust!)

You get the point. The more you put into the relationship, the more you get out of it. And with a few key questions, you'll wind up getting just what you're looking for, without even knowing in advance exactly what that's going to be.

THE SMART CUSTOMER DO'S AND DON'TS

DON'T ask, "Is this drinkable?"

I hear it all the time. It drives me nuts. A good wine guy wouldn't carry anything he thought wasn't drinkable, would he? That wouldn't be a great way to build, or even stay in, business. And think about it. Would a not-so-great wine guy tell you something was bad even if he thought it was?

DO ask, "Can you tell me something about this wine?"

DON'T say, "This can't be any good for $6.99, right?"

When I hear that question, I am quick to tell the customer that he can pay more for the bottle, if that makes him feel better about it.

DO ask if it is among the best values in the store for the price.

DON'T ask, "Can I get anything halfway decent for $25.00?"

Why would you want anything only *halfway* decent, especially for that kind of money?

DO say, "I'm looking for a (whatever). Do you have any particularly good values to recommend for around $25.00?" (And at that price, you should expect something pretty great.)

DON'T say, "I need a red wine."

DO say, "I'm looking for a something to go with lamb, somewhere in the (whatever) price range." Share whatever information you possess regarding needs and preferences. The more information you can offer regarding your likes, dislikes, pairing plans, and price range, the better.

DON'T be offended if your store doesn't carry something specific that you're looking for. They would go broke if they said yes to every winemaker that came their way.

DO ask if they carry anything similar. You might even discover something you like better. And if you're dead-set on a particular wine, ask if they can order it for you. If it's available to them, it shouldn't be a problem. Though expect to chip in and buy at least half a case to make it worth their while to special order.

Above all, **DO** ask for recommendations. In my book, the best customers are those who are always willing to try new things. They are the ones who get the most out of what I have to offer. If you don't have enough confidence in your wine guy to do this, perhaps you haven't found the right one. Keep looking. He's out there somewhere.

CHAPTER EIGHT

ASK THE WINE GUY

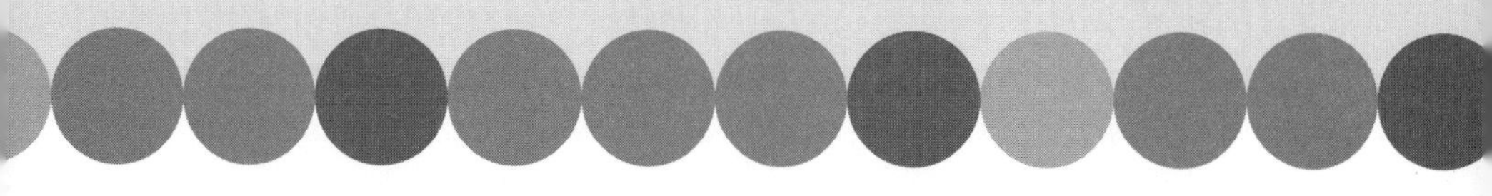

I get all sorts of challenging questions thrown at me every single day. My store is on a busy Manhattan street and the door is always open, and there I am, behind that counter, free for the asking. *Where is the Children's Museum? Can you give me change for the parking meter? Are you a notary public?* My favorite was the request for advice on zipper repair.

But most of the questions I get are good ones—ones that all of us, as wine lovers, wonder about at some point. Since your time is better spent tasting than wondering, I'll share with you the answers to the questions I'm most commonly asked.

How much does the vintage matter?

This is a fair question. The answer is that in terms of getting a good wine, not much.

The vintage year is the year of the grape harvest. A vintage's performance is more or less determined by the weather leading up to that harvest. But barring some cataclysmic meteorological event or some extraordinarily good conditions, the fluctuations between vintages (in terms of the wine quality) are usually not that huge.

In many parts of the New World wine-growing regions, the weather doesn't vary all that much, so vintage variations are relatively slight. Old World winemakers have to live with a different reality. They can be faced with huge swings in climate conditions within a single year, ranging from heat waves to cold snaps, and sometimes have to deal with horrendous rainfall, as well as hailstorms. But no matter what nature brings, they know how to use whatever is cultivated to its best advantage. Grapes from a less-than-perfect crop can be blended with grapes from another, unaffected vineyard. In truly extreme conditions, some winemakers may decide to skip the vintage altogether. One bad offering can take years to live down, and they know it.

There have been many instances where wineries have made excellent wines in a less-than-perfect vintage. Their success can come from a number of variables, including the exact location of the vineyard, the timing of the harvest, the winemakers' own unique skills, and the availability of new technological advances. So don't discount all wines from a vintage that's regarded as mediocre.

And yes, there are outstanding vintages. With perfect weather, magic can happen. But an exceptional vintage is no guarantee of an exceptional wine. It's just an indication that, due to the optimal conditions, a wine from that vintage is likely to be at its best.

So how do you know when and where this magic occurred? Was 1997 considered a good year in Tuscany? What was 2001 like in California? Take it to the experts. Use a vintage chart, which can be found in wine magazines and online. They can come in handy in restaurants, or when you're in pursuit of older, rarer vintages as gifts or perhaps for your own collection.

Obviously, all vintages do have an end. Great ones are rare, and they disappear quickly once the word is out. So if you find a wine you really, really love from a highly rated vintage, buy it while it lasts. Just be prepared to eventually get over it and move on. If you can't find that special vintage you're looking for, give the next year's a try. Even though it may not have received the same hype, odds are you'll be satisfied.

Do you have a Champagne in the $10-to-$15 range?

Sorry, no. In order for any sparkler to be called Champagne, it must come from the Champagne region in France, and that's where the big bucks (more like $25 and up) come into play. But not every occasion calls for "real" Champagne. If you are open to a sparkling wine, then your options are much broader. All bubbly made outside of the Champagne region is categorized as sparkling wine. In fact, today only one out of every twelve bottles of bubbly produced comes from Champagne.

Champagne is made from various combinations of three grapes—Pinot Meunier, Pinot Noir, and Chardonnay. Most are a combination of all three, with the exceptions of the softer, richer, and creamier Blanc de Noirs (made from the two Pinots) and the lighter, crisper, more delicate Blanc de Blancs (solely from the Chardonnay grape.) Rosé Champagnes tend to be fuller in body than the others, and are more expensive due to limited production.

The most prevalent and most affordable Champagnes are non-vintage—blends of still wines from a number of different vintages. But when an exceptional year comes along, vintage Champagnes are made. In order to be designated vintage and display the actual vintage year on the label, a Champagne must be made with at least 80 percent of the wine coming from that one harvest. Since not every year is vintage-worthy, the price of vintage Champagne is about double that of non-vintage. But you can definitely taste the difference.

Vintage Champagnes can age well for up to ten years. Since you won't know when non-vintage Champagnes were actually bottled, to be safe you should drink them within five years of purchase (ideally sooner). In any event, store Champagne as you would any wine. And don't follow the common practice of "storing" it forever in the fridge. That's a no-no. As with any wine, long-term extreme cold will flatten the flavors. And *never* put a bottle of bubbly in the freezer. It will explode. Trust me, I've done it. Instead, place it in a bucket of ice-cold water.

When shopping for Champagne, you'll run across five different classifications, which are based on the level of sweetness. The sweetness comes from sugar that is added just prior to the final bottling. *Brut* is the driest, the most common, and the style reserved for the Champagne maker's best blend, or *cuvée. Extra dry* is slightly sweeter. *Demi-sec* is medium sweet, *sec* sweeter still, and *doux*, very sweet and very rare.

Every winemaking country in the world makes its own version of a sparkler. And choosing to go with sparkling wine instead of Champagne does not mean that you have to compromise your standards. There are plenty of delicious sparkling wines that you can enjoy without breaking the bank.

Cava is a sparkling wine that's made in Northern Spain from the Xarel-lo, Parellada, Macabeo, and Chardonnay grapes. Unfortunately, they don't age as well as Champagne grapes, but the wines are yummy when enjoyed young and are a fraction of the cost.

From Italy, there's Prosecco from the Veneto region. Made from the Prosecco grape, these wines are just slightly sparkling, or *frizzante*. There are other spumantes (Italian for "sparkling") coming from all over Italy, most notably Asti, Lambrusco, and Franciacorta.

In the United States there are some terrific sparklers from Washington, New York, and most notably California, where a few labels are owned by famous Champagne houses. There's even an excellent bubbly from New Mexico called Gruet. Many others can be found from Australia (whites *and* reds), Germany (called *sekt*), and French regions outside of Champagne, and a few are being made in South America and South Africa.

Do you have any inexpensive cooking wine?

Don't get me started on this one. I'm a firm believer that the better the wine that goes into the food, the better the final outcome. You've bought an expensive piece of meat or fish and you want to sauce it, braise it, and marinate it with the cheapest thing you can find? I'm not saying you should whip out a Chassagne-Montrachet or a Pomerol and dowse your dinner in it; just stay away from the "It's only for cooking so it needn't be any good" concept. Even though the alcohol burns off, the flavors of the wine will come through. Meet yourself halfway and get something that you would like to sip while making that lovely meal. There will always be a glass left over once you've added a cup or two to the dish.

Recipes often call for a "dry white." My advice is most any white will do. I tend to recommend Sauvignon Blanc, Chenin Blanc, or Pinot Grigio. Stay away from big, bold whites like California Chardonnays—you're not looking to change the flavor of the food, you just want to enhance it. With reds, use a big wine, like a Bordeaux or a Cabernet Sauvignon, if it's beef you're making. Poultry calls for a lighter touch, such as a Pinot Noir.

As far as I'm concerned, the best thing to do is use the same wine you'll be drinking with the meal. The same principles apply to pairing for cooking as to pairing for dining.

Do you have any Boxed Wine?

Last summer, a well-dressed, silver-haired man entered my shop, asking for box twine. Considering what I'd been asked at times, the question didn't really surprise me. I directed the man to a hardware store down the street.

"*That's* not very funny," he replied, before storming out the door.

I didn't get it. For once, I wasn't trying to be funny.

"I think he wanted boxed wine," came the voice of one of my staff from the back of the store, too late. I was mortified. I pursued the man for a block and apologized profusely, explaining my mistake and, since I did not carry any boxed wine, pointed him toward a competitor who did. He never even cracked a smile.

I now do carry a couple of boxed wines—a terrific Trebbiano from Italy, and a yummy Languedoc red. I really don't have a problem with the concept. On the contrary. The "bag-in-a-box" system that's widely used today offers a long-lasting (the bags are airtight), resealable (wines remain fresh for at least a month after the spigot is opened), and cheap (no expensive glass bottles) alternative. In France, le "bag-in-a-box" is even marketed as a good solution for older people who have trouble opening bottles. I've seen trunkfuls of boxes flying out of wineries and tasting rooms there.

Most Americans still equate boxes with lower-quality, high-volume wines, and in this country that's still pretty much the case. In Australia, boxed wines have been wildly popular for years, and some of their higher-quality ones are making their way here. A few California wineries have started to follow their lead. If the trend continues, I'll be happy to stack lots of those boxes on my shelves, and I'll never have to humiliate myself in front of a cube-craving customer again.

What's up with the fake cork?

Some synthetic corks are okay. Using plastic in place of natural cork helps to keep wines from becoming "corked." However, some synthetic corks have been found to have problems with leakage, odor, and extraction. And if you can get them *back* into the bottle, you're a genius. In terms of how wines age with synthetic corks, nothing has been proven yet. I know some winemakers who have stopped using them altogether, while others are giving them more of a chance. But stay tuned. Time will tell.

What, *no* cork?

Don't be misled. Screw caps are no longer necessarily a sign of a cheap or lousy wine. In fact, many respectable winemakers, particularly in Australia and New Zealand, have embraced this tried-and-true practice. Several major California wineries are now bottling premium wines with screw caps. Even France is starting to join in.

Why? No cork means no cork taint, no oxidation, and no spoilage . . . guaranteed.

So don't judge your wine by its stopper. Don't let snobbery get in your way. I spend a lot of time convincing customers that the screw cap is just fine, in fact better than fine, and that they'd better get used to it. Screw caps are here to stay.

Can I return this bottle?

Luckily, this question isn't all that common at West Side Wine, but if you get a bad bottle, you're entitled to an exchange. However, occasionally people try to return a bottle just because they didn't like the wine. This really isn't a legitimate reason to ask for something else. You wouldn't return a half-eaten box of cookies because you found them too buttery, would you?

So if you think it's the bottle and not the wine (check the color, odor, and taste for oxidation, or sniff it and sip it if you suspect cork taint), take it back as soon as you can (ideally within a couple of days), and get an opinion from your salesperson. The longer you wait, the less likely it is that you'll get an exchange. If the open bottle sits around too long, it will be difficult to make an accurate assessment. If it is oxidized or corked, your wine seller should take it back and offer another bottle. It's no big deal for sellers to do so, as they can get a credit from the distributor who sold it to them in the first place. So nobody will lose and, most important, you'll be satisfied.

Should I let this wine breathe?

Most wines don't really need to breathe deeply. The oxygen they're exposed to while in the glass is plenty to allow them to aerate. There is one exception: full-bodied reds, when they're young and haven't yet reached their full flavor, will really benefit when given more exposure to air. Now, that doesn't mean just taking the cork out of the bottle and letting it sit for a while. Doing that only exposes that tiny bit of wine at the top of the bottle neck to oxygen. You can let the genie out of the bottle by using a decanter. The wine will breathe while it is flowing into the decanter, and will continue its magic while it basks in the open air.

It's wise to use a decanter as well with older full-bodied reds, as there is often sediment at the bottom of the bottle. Sediment is simply a natural separation of "stuff" from the grapes. But it doesn't taste great, so you'll want to avoid it. Slowly pour the wine from the bottle into the decanter. With any luck, the sediment will stay in the bottle and won't end up in your mouth.

In most cases, the decanting process won't hurt a wine. But it can sometimes destroy a really, *really* old bottle. Once a wine is decades old, it probably has already reached its max in terms of opening up. When it hits the air, this exposure can be the final straw, and it may simply fall apart.

In choosing a decanter, there's no need to worry about the

"right" kind. It's all a matter of aesthetics. All decanters are designed to properly aerate the wine. Go with what you like.

Should I serve this chilled?

Here's my opinion on serving temperature: 99 percent of the American wine-consuming public drink their whites too cold and their reds too warm.

I see it with my customers all the time. They beg for speedy deliveries, assuming their whites need hours of fridge time before a party. Wrong. Stick those whites in an hour before serving; otherwise they'll taste like a cold nothing. All the nuances and subtleties will disappear in the deep freeze. If you do have wine that's been chilling forever, take it out a half hour before serving time to let it warm up a little. And don't store your whites long-term in the refrigerator, unless you truly have no other option.

Don't be afraid to put a red in the fridge if it's too warm. Heat brings out that burning sensation that alcohol imparts to wine, and you don't want that. How can you tell if a red needs a chill? If the bottle doesn't feel slightly cool in your hand, it's too warm. Stick it in the fridge for about twenty minutes to cool it off.

What about ice plunked into a wineglass? I'm no snob, but I have trained many a relative to never ask me for ice unless they're drinking water. It melts, it dilutes the wine's flavor, and it changes everything. It's a no-no in my house.

Does it make any difference what glass I use?

This whole wineglass thing has gotten way out of hand. Do we actually need a different-shaped glass for every grape? I think not.

Unless you've got a kitchen the size of Julia Child's, and a wallet the size of Rockefeller's, you might want to consider this: you really can get away with just one set of wineglasses. A twelve-ounce glass should do the trick for both reds and whites—it's big enough for you to have room to swirl, and for those yummy aromas to gather.

It's best to use glasses that bulge out down below and curve in at the rim. The widest part of the glass will allow a good portion of the wine to be exposed to air (fill the glass only to that point), and the narrow top will capture the scents. A thin rim is preferable. You'll hardly know it's there, so you won't be distracted from concentrating on the wine. And stay away from colored glasses, as pretty as they look. Seeing the color of the wine is part of the tasting experience, remember?

Most wineglasses have stems, the thought being that if you hold the stem, then the wine will be protected from becoming warmed by your hands. Now stemless wineglasses are starting to appear on the horizon. In fact, in the Old World, people have been drinking out of tumblers forever. Stems or not, either will work just fine.

If you are a fan of Champagnes and sparkling wines, then you *do* need a separate set of glasses. The traditional options are the flute style and the saucer style (the latter, according to legend, having been designed from a mold of Marie Antoinette's breasts!). I recommend the flute. With less room for the bubbles to escape, the flute keeps the bubbly bubbly.

Whatever you do, don't spend too much, so it doesn't become a tragedy if you or your friends let a glass slip to the floor. And you will. And if you have money left over? Buy another set. I'd suggest a larger size for red—eighteen ounces or bigger. Bigger wines benefit from bigger glasses.

Once the party is over, and it's time to clean up, go light with the soap. Rinse well. A soapy odor or taste doesn't exactly enhance the flavor of wine.

Is this ready to drink now?

Most wines today are made to be consumed immediately. Only a small percentage of people buy wine to "lay it down."

There are certainly wines that evolve and improve with age. But even if a wine is known to age well, that's not to say you can't drink it now. It won't be bad. There is a time for everything, though, and wines can pass their prime. So if you are planning on hiding away some special bottles for the distant future, ask your wine seller how long they'll last.

What's the best way to store my wines?

Keeping some extra bottles around the house is a good thing to do, if you have the room. Say you find a wine you love, and perhaps it's one that won't be available for long. Bring a bunch home! If your wine seller gives significant discounts for buying by the case, take advantage of the offer. You hate to shop? Buy more, shop less!

But that doesn't mean you need to have an extensive, expensive wine cellar. All you need to do is follow three simple rules:

1. Keep It Cool

You don't want to cook your wine. A warm temperature will make wine age faster, and a truly hot environment will damage it. The ideal "cellar" temperature is 55 to 60 degrees Fahrenheit, but don't get too crazy about it—you do have a little leeway.

2. Keep It Dark

Do not put your wine near windows, or under the constant glare of ultraviolet or fluorescent light. Light (especially direct sunlight, due to the heat factor) can prematurely age wine. Wine can also become "light struck"—a condition that makes it taste sort of like wet cardboard.

3. Keep It Constant

Temperature fluctuations are the worst thing that you can put a wine through. They can cause the wine to expand and contract, which causes a pushing and pulling on the cork, which in turn can compromise the seal and allow oxygen to enter.

With these rules in mind, think about your alternatives. Kitchens are a bad place to store your wine. They're the hottest rooms in the house. Basements are great, on all three counts. Plus they're slightly damp, which will help keep the corks from drying out. If you don't have a basement, how about the bottom of a closet? It's perfectly acceptable. Get rid of those old shoes and make way for the wine.

If you can keep the bottles on their sides, do so. This will keep the corks from drying out and shrinking. Simple wine racks do a great job. And temperature-controlled storage units (they look like little fridges) are becoming more and more affordable. You just need to have enough room for them.

If you do start amassing a collection, try to keep track of what you've got, and drink it before it's too late. Older isn't necessarily better. Most wines are made to be consumed within a couple of years of production. Remember what you've been taught about your grapes, and stay aware of which ones improve with age, and which don't.

Can wine keep in an open bottle?

Now, you may not want to hear this, but when you open a bottle of wine, you don't have to drink it all. "It might go bad" is no longer a good excuse for draining the bottle. Today there are excellent, inexpensive solutions for home storage of opened bottles.

Remember, oxygen changes the way wine tastes, so if you like what you are tasting, keep it that way. The most effective methods of storage involve extracting the oxygen from the bottle or preventing contact between the wine and the oxygen.

The first is done with a little hand pump and a rubber stopper. The other is accomplished by spraying a nitrogen and carbon dioxide gas into the bottle, which does not affect the wine's taste. If you don't have one of those devices, invest in one now. They're cheap, and you'll be saving money by not tossing out ruined wine. Until then, you can simply put the cork back in the bottle or use a regular old bottle stopper. Keep your leftover bottles cool (put them in the fridge) and don't let them stay left over too long—finish them off within two or three days.

If none of this works for you, think about buying half bottles. Although they're not half the price, they may end up being more economical if the alternative is throwing out a lot of wine.

Wine is supposed to be good for you, right?

Well, that's what they say. Even Louis Pasteur said, "Wine is the most healthful and hygienic of beverages." Probably the best-known claim is that red wine reduces the incidence of heart disease. A scientist named Serge Renaud triggered a boom in California wine sales in 1991 when he brought forth the notion of what has been coined "The French Paradox"—the fact that the French could smoke like chimneys and eat so much rich, creamy food without keeling over right and left from heart attacks. His theory? It's all in the wine. And many other studies have since backed him up. There now seems to be no arguing with the fact that moderate wine consumption is associated with lower coronary heart disease mortality.

It's not the alcohol that does the trick. Health benefits from wine (including improved brain function!) have been linked to red wine's antioxidant properties. The component resveratrol, in particular, has been shown to have an anti-clotting effect that can help prevent heart attack and strokes, and has also been demonstrated to have anti-cancer effects. Other evidence suggests that it could be useful in treating symptoms of serious lung disease. And recently scientists at the University of California, Davis, identified a group of chemicals called saponins in red wine, which have been linked to the ability to lower cholesterol.

So yes, wine can be good for you. But only in moderation. Researchers have found that those who drink one to three glasses a day are healthier than both those who drink none and those who drink more.

I'm allergic to sulfites. Are there any wines that don't have them?

All wines contain sulfites. Sulfites are natural compounds produced by the yeasts used during the fermentation process, and (contrary to popular belief) they're not all bad. Sulfites are antioxidants and work to fight off bacteria, thus acting as a natural preservative, allowing wines to age longer and reach their proper maturity.

Here's the problem: because of these beneficial properties, practically all winemakers *add* sulfites to their wines. It's their insurance that their wines won't "turn" before their time.

Many people believe that Old World wines are sulfite-free. Not true! This misconception probably comes from the fact that wine sold in other parts of the world doesn't carry the "contains sulfites" warning that is required on bottles sold in the United States. The fact is that Europe has been adding sulfites to their wines since the seventeenth century. The use of added sulfites actually dates back to the times of the Romans and the Egyptians, when they were used to clean wine vats.

Unfortunately, approximately one in one hundred people are allergic to sulfites. Asthmatics are particularly susceptible. Symptoms range from skin rashes, hives, wheezing, and breathing difficulties to gastrointestinal disorders such as nausea and stomach cramps. There is a common belief that sulfites cause headaches, but that has been proven unlikely.

If you are sensitive to sulfites, there are a couple of ways to minimize exposure that you should know about. White wines and dessert wines have more sulfites than red wines, so sticking to reds might help. There are also so-called sulfite-free wines available—wines that fall within the Bureau of Alcohol, Tobacco and Firearms' definition of having sulfite levels of less than ten parts per million. Those wines are not required to carry the "contains sulfites" label. Badger Mountain and Frey Vineyards are two of the American wineries known for their "sulfite-free" wines.

Keep in mind that sulfites are preservatives. Wines with low levels of sulfites need to be consumed young, usually within a year to eighteen months of bottling. After that, you'll run the risk of being disappointed by a tired, if not dead, bottle of wine.

What's the difference between an organic wine and a "sulfite-free" wine?

Organic wines are made from organically grown grapes. This means that no chemical pesticides, fertilizers, or fungicides are used in the grape-growing process, and that no cultured yeasts are used in the fermentation process. Filtration and clarifying (or "fining") are kept to a minimum.

But "organic" does not mean sulfite-free. Although most truly organic winemakers choose to (or in some cases are required to) limit or avoid adding sulfites, wines made organically *can* have as many sulfites as wines made in the conventional way.

More and more winemakers are opting to grow organically, for the sake of soil preservation and other ecological concerns. Why not eliminate those nasty chemicals if at all possible? Think about it: organic winemaking was the only way to make wine before chemical enhancers were invented.

But the market remains limited, and many organic winemakers are reluctant to position or label their wines as organic, fearing the stigma that is often attached to "health foods" and other things that are supposedly good for you. Some stores do feature a separate "organic" section, but in many cases you will have to rely on the knowledge of your retailer to point you to the right bottles. In terms of taste, there actually is not much detectable difference, other than perhaps a richer flavor that can result from the lack of filtering and fining.

If you want to go the organic route, you should be aware that organic wines can cost more than non-organically made wines. The process is labor intensive and, as a result, comparatively smaller amounts are made. Also remember that, as they may contain a lower level of sulfites, organic wines sometimes have a shorter shelf life. If you don't see the "contains sulfites" indication on the label, drink them now.

How come I don't get headaches when I drink wine in Italy?

Many people who are prone to wine headaches make the claim that wines from certain parts of the world are more tolerable than others. Who knows? That could be true, for them. The fact is that not a lot of research has been done on the topic of headaches and wine.

We do know this: headaches can occur from drinking too much wine—the good old-fashioned hangover. Aside from over-imbibing, the presence of histamine or tyramine in red wines could be the problem. They can cause what is known as the "red wine headache syndrome," commonly referred to as RWH (no kidding!). Another trigger, for those prone to migraines, may be tannins.

But these may not be the only contributing factors. Everyone has a unique physiology, and therefore unique sensitivities. If you do suffer from RWH, don't give up. Do some experimenting and find out if there are any particular grapes or regions that are kinder to you. You might try taking aspirin before drinking red wine, or try an antihistamine to counter negative effects. And if being on an overseas vacation seems to allow you unlimited enjoyment without paying a price, did you ever consider the psychological factor?

What wine will go with my dinner?

Food and wine complement each other, either by mirroring the other's flavors or by contrasting them. While each may taste good individually, they'll absolutely taste better together.

The pairing of wine and food has itself become an entire topic of study. With the abundance of choices in wine out there, attitudes have changed. These days, the school of thought is that just about anything goes. The red-with-meat and white-with-fish thing is over. Now wine and food pairing really comes down to personal preference and a little common sense. Knowing what you've already learned about your grapes, you can use taste and logic to determine which wines will bring out the best in a meal and what meal will bring out the best in a wine. I'll give you a head start on the logic part.

1. Stay in your weight class. Think body. Delicate foods will be squashed under a heavyweight wine. Conversely, a steak will swat away a light-bodied wine as though it were an annoying gnat. No contest, in either event.
2. When you're dealing with qualities like richness and acidity, either go with the flow or swim against the tide. For example, rich, creamy foods can be paired with an equally rich, low-acidity, full-bodied wine. But if you want to counteract the rich food with a high-acidity, crisper wine, then go ahead. It's your call, because both work. The same goes for a high-acidity food,

like a tomato-based dish, where you can mirror or contrast the acidity with a wine from either end of the scale.

3. With salty or spicy foods, you may want to think about a fruitier, less acidic wine to balance the intensity.
4. Most often, a wine from a particular region will go well with traditional food from that region. The reason for that goes way back to the time when wine wasn't made for export; it was made to go with whatever the locals were eating. Over the years, those "local" wines have been perfected, and they are now exported and enjoyed all over the world.

As you experiment with all kinds of food pairings, you're bound to luck out with many ideal couplings. The most important thing is to keep your mind and options open, drink what you like, and make your own pairing discoveries. Then pass them on to a friend.

What's good to bring as a gift?

Ah, the gift of wine! It's always an appropriate gesture. (Alas, no one brings it to *my* house anymore . . . not since I've become the Wine Guy.) But what to choose for that special someone, or that special occasion? My philosophy is simple:

1. In general, choose a red. Unless, of course, you know that the recipient absolutely doesn't drink red wine.
2. Don't overspend—it's not about what you spend, it's about how well you choose. And if you choose well, your recipient will think you spent *much* more than you actually did.
3. Be courageous—give them something they've probably never tried before. Offering the unusual shows that you gave the situation some thought. And besides, if they're not familiar with the wine, they *really* won't know what it cost.

4. As an alternative to a red, pick out a sparkling wine. One can always use a bottle of bubbly in the house for those unexpected celebratory occasions.
5. Are you bringing wine to be consumed with lunch or dinner? If so, ask what your hosts are planning on serving. If you don't know, try to bring something medium-bodied that goes well with lots of different foods, such as a Pinot Noir, a Chianti, or a Rioja.
6. For something unique, bring a dessert wine or a fortified wine (port or sherry). This is an easy way to complement any meal, and an easy way to get credit for doing something different.

What's the etiquette about serving a bottle a guest brought . . . or not?

Our friend Rosie has some neighbors who always bring the same bottle of Pinot Grigio whenever they come over. Neither Rosie nor her partner can stand the stuff, but they feel funny about not opening it.

My advice? Thank your neighbors for the gesture, put that bottle in the kitchen, and leave it there. Tell them you have a special wine you'd like them to try, and serve your own.

On the other hand, my friend Cliff was once a guest at a San Francisco dinner celebrating the opening of Dungeness crab season. He carefully selected a pricey bottle of Viognier from his collection, salivating over the thought of how it would complement the richness of the succulent crab, but the bottle was spirited away by his hosts, never to be seen again. Instead, he was asked if he would prefer a generic "white" or "red" with his dinner.

Come on, man! Speak up! Tell your hosts you brought that wine specifically because you thought it would go great with the food, and suggest you all try it to see if your hunch was right.

I'm having a party. How much wine do I need?

Party time! And a good question. It would be a shame to run out of wine, but on the other hand, you don't want to break the bank. To answer this one, there are a few things to consider, besides the obvious matter of how many people will be attending.

What's the length of your party? What type of event is it? A cocktail party? Are you planning on serving liquor and other beverages in addition to the wine? Is it cocktails, then dinner? Just dinner? Are there any children figured into the guest count?

As a rule, for a regular two-hour cocktail party, factoring in hard liquor and other beverages that will be available, I recommend eight regular-size (750ml) bottles of wine per twenty adults. While two 5½-ounce glasses per person may not sound like much, that's really not the way it will work out in the end. Consider that not everyone will be drinking wine, some will drink less, and some will drink more. Caterers usually figure one drink per person per hour, with the norm being two drinks the first hour and then a slowing down to one drink an hour thereafter. There can always be surprises, but I've found that this formula usually works out well, with maybe just a little left over for future occasions.

And what about the ratio of white to red? That's a little tougher. If you don't know what your guests prefer, go a little heavier on the whites. I've found that more white than red gets consumed at an average cocktail party. For an indoor party on an average-weather night, I'd recommend you make five of those eight bottles white; on a hot, steamy night, six out of eight.

For parties where a meal is being served, you'll need to calculate a little more per person, as you probably won't be offering other beverage options. Figure two to three glasses (around a half bottle) per person to play it safe.

If it's drinks, then dinner? Go easy on the "before" wine. One glass per person, or less if you're offering other cocktails, should be enough.

How can I get a red wine stain out?

I'm certainly no expert on cleaning, but the two most common pieces of advice that I've come across on this matter involve a homemade solution of hydrogen peroxide and Dawn liquid soap, or the commercially available Wine Away. Lots of luck! Most of my customers with white furniture and/or white rugs don't buy red wine for any large gathering.

CHAPTER NINE

BECOMING YOUR OWN WINE GUY

My California brother-in-law loves having a wine guy in the family. He's always calling from restaurants to read me the wine list and ask what I think will go best with his dinner. When I visit, he spirits me away in his car to Napa and Sonoma, charging me with filling the trunk with a supply that will last until my next trip west. He flies east every year expressly to sample the goods at our annual wine party. He wouldn't miss it for the world.

Once he reads this book, he won't need me anymore. And neither will you. If you've gotten this far, you not only have the skills to communicate your preferences to your wine guy, you have what it takes to start deciphering labels to make some picks on your own. You're also ready to apply your knowledge to enjoying the wine experience at restaurants, wine bars, wineries, and wine events. You could even throw your own wine party, or start your own wine club! All you need to do is approach each situation with the same confidence and sense of adventure that you take with you when you shop for wine.

GOING IT ALONE

Deciphering a label is one of the most common challenges faced by wine shoppers everywhere. But it's not all that difficult, once you know what you're looking for.

A wine label contains all the clues you need to determine whether or not what's in the bottle is something you might want. All you have to do is locate the clues and apply that information to what you've learned about your own personal preferences.

What do you look for first? The grape.

WHERE'S THE GRAPE?

Sometimes finding the grape will be easy, particularly when the wine is a varietal—named for the dominant grape from which it is made. You'll find this most often with wines from New World countries, along with Alsatian, German, and Austrian wines. In the United States, the grape has to represent 75 percent or more of a blend for this to be allowed.

Then there are wines that use a proprietary name, like Caymus Conundrum, Cline Red Truck, or Bonny Doon Big House Red. Wines with made-up names from New World blends usually have the grapes listed somewhere on the label. Rarely do you see them listed on Old World blends with made-up names. If you don't know what's in the bottle, ask.

Most Old World wines, particularly ones from France, Italy, and Spain, are named for the region in which the grapes are grown (a.k.a. the appellation). Often the grapes will not be listed, so it helps to know what grapes are grown where. The good news is that things do seem to be easing up in terms of how appellation wines can and can't be labeled, specifically in France, where winemakers are starting to include grape names so their wines will be more easily marketable.

HOW'S THE BODY?

You've already narrowed down the range for body by picking your grape. Now check the alcohol level, found on every label, to see where the wine fits within that range.

Remember: light-bodied wines range from 7 to 10.5 percent alcohol, medium from 10.5 to 13 percent, and full at higher than 13 percent.

IS IT MY STYLE?

The first thing to look at is where the wine was made. Think of how geography affects style. Though there are some exceptions (those winemakers who are crossing over with technique), this is usually a good hint.

Next, see if there are any descriptive words on either the front or back label that provide other pieces to the puzzle. You may find clues like "barrel fermented," which tells you that the wine was not just aged in oak, it was fermented in oak as well, and therefore will taste more oaky. "Un-oaked" is also a style indicator often found right on the label. On top of these hints, you might also come across actual flavor and aroma descriptors to help lead the way. Some winemakers will describe growing conditions and their effects on flavor and style, and some might suggest food pairings. Don't ignore what's on the back of the bottle. It could come in handy.

Once you get past all that, and you should be able to without much problem, you may want to check out some of the information that relates to the quality of the wine. If you don't see these indicators, it doesn't mean the wine isn't any good. It's additional information that lets you know what the wine is all about.

Appellation

You already may have looked to appellation as a clue to what grapes you're getting. But the designation of an appellation tells you more than that. With Old World wines, it's your guarantee that the winemakers have adhered to strict regulations—what grapes can be used, what techniques are allowed, and more—designed to protect the traditions of their region and to ensure a certain level of quality. The following letters on a label are a sign of a wine that meets the standards of its region.

FRANCE:	AOC or AC (Appellation d'Origine Côntrolée)
GERMANY:	QmP (Qualitätswein mit Pradikat)
ITALY:	DOC (Denominazione di Origine Controllata)
PORTUGAL:	DOC (Denominacão de Origem Controlada)
SPAIN:	DO (Denominación de Origen)

In the United States, appellation (AVA—American Viticultural Area) is solely an indication of growing region. Regulations relating to other aspects of growing and making the wine don't exist here.

Vintage

This is a quality clue if you know what's what. Keep those vintage charts handy, if you're curious.

Estate Bottled

This means that the grapes were 100-percent grown, plus vinified and bottled, in the same place. What that means to you is that the winemaker is taking full responsibility for quality, and that usually puts them a cut above. Sometimes the label will say *Estate Grown* or *Chateau Bottled* . . . same thing. Just don't mix it up with *Bot-*

tled By or *Produced and Bottled By* or *Made and Bottled By*—if it doesn't indicate "estate" or "chateau," they're missing at least one part of the equation.

And in other countries? In France, look for the words *Mis en Bouteille* ("put in bottle") *au Château* or *au Domaine* or *au Mas*. The Italians say *Imbottigliato All'Origine*, and in Germany it's *Gutsabfüllung* or *Erzeugerabfüllung*. Spanish winemakers seem to usually use the English *Estate Bottled*, but sometimes I see *Embotellado en la Propriedad*.

Reserve

Be careful about this one. In Spain (*Reserva*) and Italy (*Riserva*), winemakers must adhere to certain minimum aging requirements in order to label their wines this way. But in the United States, *Reserve* is a subjective designation given to the wine by the winemaker. Sometimes it's used to indicate something they consider to be a special blend, or to show that the grapes come from a special vineyard, but there are no legal qualifications for using that word on a label. So how do you know whether it's an indication of an honest opinion, or simply a sales gimmick? Tough call.

Old Vines/Vieille Vignes

This is just what it says. And the older, the better. If well cared for, those mature vines will be pushing out some pretty high-quality grapes.

Low Yield

Another indication of quality. The fewer vines planted, the more they benefit from what the soil has to offer.

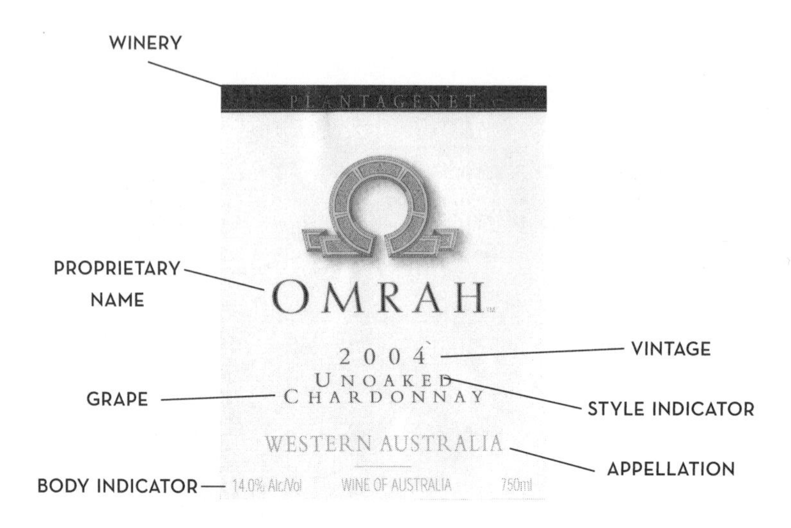
WINERY
PLANTAGENET
PROPRIETARY NAME
OMRAH
2004
VINTAGE
UNOAKED
CHARDONNAY
GRAPE
STYLE INDICATOR
WESTERN AUSTRALIA
APPELLATION
BODY INDICATOR
14.0% Alc/Vol
WINE OF AUSTRALIA
750ml

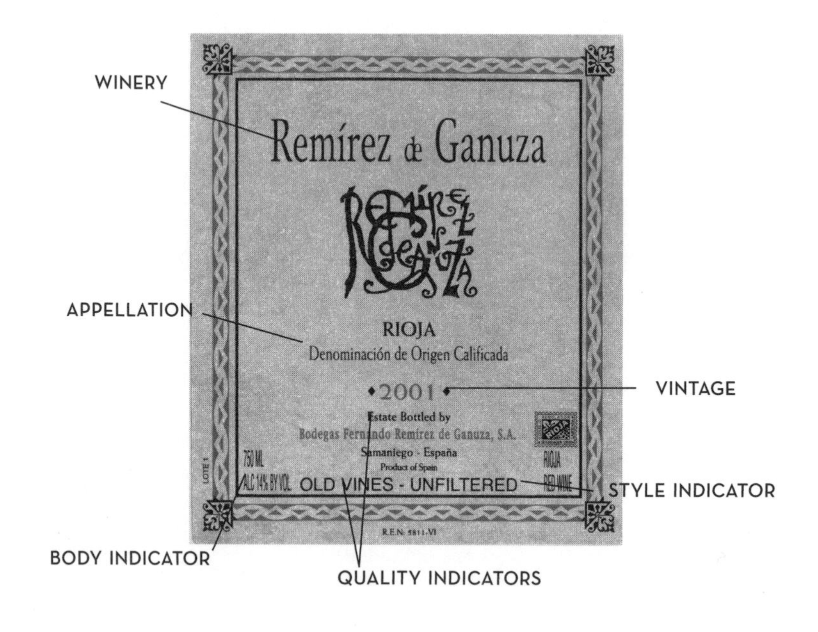
WINERY
Remírez de Ganuza
APPELLATION
RIOJA
Denominación de Origen Calificada
2001
VINTAGE
Estate Bottled by
Bodegas Fernando Remírez de Ganuza, S.A.
Samaniego - España
Product of Spain
750 ML
ALC 14% BY VOL
OLD VINES - UNFILTERED
RIOJA
RED WINE
STYLE INDICATOR
R.E.N. 5811-VI
BODY INDICATOR
QUALITY INDICATORS

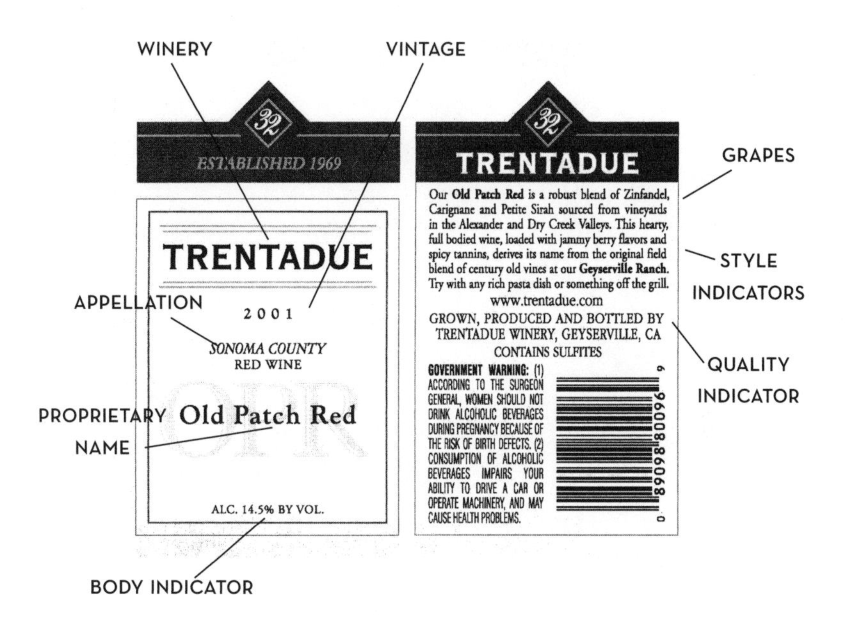
WINERY
VINTAGE
ESTABLISHED 1969
TRENTADUE
APPELLATION
2001
SONOMA COUNTY
RED WINE
PROPRIETARY NAME
Old Patch Red
ALC. 14.5% BY VOL.
BODY INDICATOR
TRENTADUE
GRAPES
Our Old Patch Red is a robust blend of Zinfandel, Carignane and Petite Sirah sourced from vineyards in the Alexander and Dry Creek Valleys. This hearty, full bodied wine, loaded with jammy berry flavors and spicy tannins, derives its name from the original field blend of century old vines at our Geyserville Ranch. Try with any rich pasta dish or something off the grill.
STYLE INDICATORS
www.trentadue.com
GROWN, PRODUCED AND BOTTLED BY TRENTADUE WINERY, GEYSERVILLE, CA
CONTAINS SULFITES
QUALITY INDICATOR
GOVERNMENT WARNING: (1) ACCORDING TO THE SURGEON GENERAL, WOMEN SHOULD NOT DRINK ALCOHOLIC BEVERAGES DURING PREGNANCY BECAUSE OF THE RISK OF BIRTH DEFECTS. (2) CONSUMPTION OF ALCOHOLIC BEVERAGES IMPAIRS YOUR ABILITY TO DRIVE A CAR OR OPERATE MACHINERY, AND MAY CAUSE HEALTH PROBLEMS.
0 89098 80096 6

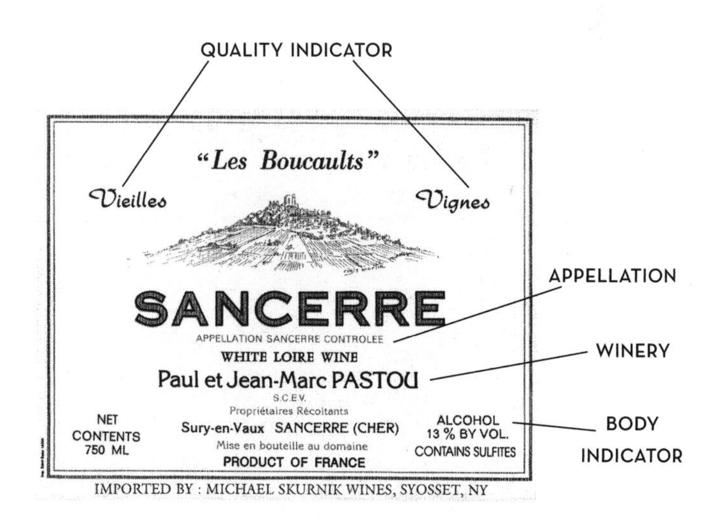
QUALITY INDICATOR
"Les Boucaults"
Vieilles Vignes
APPELLATION
SANCERRE
APPELLATION SANCERRE CONTROLEE
WHITE LOIRE WINE
WINERY
Paul et Jean-Marc PASTOU
S.C.E.V.
Propriétaires Récoltants
Sury-en-Vaux SANCERRE (CHER)
Mise en bouteille au domaine
PRODUCT OF FRANCE
NET CONTENTS 750 ML
ALCOHOL 13 % BY VOL.
CONTAINS SULFITES
BODY INDICATOR
IMPORTED BY : MICHAEL SKURNIK WINES, SYOSSET, NY

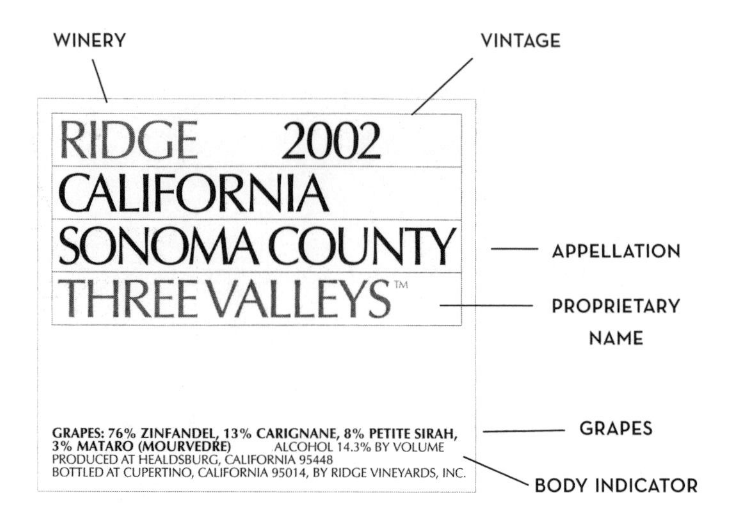

DINNER FOR THREE 

There are certain restaurants my wife won't set foot in . . . at least not with me. She refuses to go to those places with wine lists the size of phone books, because I spend too much time studying the wine choices.

Although restaurants are great places for new wine discoveries, and offer a perfect opportunity to apply what you've learned about your personal preferences, sometimes it seems difficult to make a choice. What methods have you used to make a wine selection in a restaurant? Are you the "go to the middle of the price range" type? Or the "Phew! . . . there's one I've heard of" guy? Do you close your eyes and point? Is asking for help a last resort?

Not anymore. It's the end of rash decisions, wasted opportunities, and impatient companions. You know what you like. Think about what you've learned about finding wine in a store. The same principles apply when choosing wine in a restaurant.

Imagine you're at a nice restaurant with a nice companion, only this time I'm there with you, at your service. Questions on how to deal with it all? Just ask the Wine Guy.

I think I'd like something before dinner. Any suggestions?
Ask what is available by the glass. You already know you don't want anything that's going to kill your taste buds for the rest of the afternoon or evening, so think about going with something on the light side, or perhaps some bubbly. And don't forget to express any specific preferences, in terms of grape, body, style, or flavors, to the waiter.

This wine list is huge! Where do I start?
Ignore it. Yes, I said you can ignore it. Especially if it is huge. In fact, the bigger the list, the more investment the restaurant has probably made in it, and the better chance you'll have of getting some good help with it. And help is what you should get. Ask the waiter if he is familiar with the list. If he isn't, or if he doesn't seem too sure about it, ask to speak to the person who knows it best.

Here comes the sommelier. Should I ask her for help?
Absolutely. Helping you select a wine and pointing out unusual gems on the list is a part of her job, and probably her favorite part of it. She has handpicked the restaurant's wine collection, is proud of it, and will be proud to share her knowledge. Her success comes from your enjoyment.

Above all, don't be embarrassed around a sommelier or a waitperson, and don't pretend to know what you can't possibly know. Most people can't navigate a wine list today. Just like the best wine stores, the best restaurant wine lists are full of unknowns. With new treasures becoming available every day, and with up-and-coming regions producing world-class wines, how could anyone possibly keep up?

Unfortunately, sommeliers are a rare breed these days—victims of tough restaurant economics. On the flip side, many restaurant owners are putting more emphasis on wine training for their wait staffs than ever before. They often bring in winemakers or distributor representatives, who familiarize the staff with their product. The staff tastes, and they're given guidance regarding food pairings. And they are encouraged to share that information with you.

So what do I say to her?

You know what to do. Use the wine-shopping skills you learned from this book. Tell her what you're planning on eating, and tell her what you like, either in terms of flavors, grapes, or other wines. Finally, tell her the maximum that you want to spend. Don't hesitate—it's done all the time and is a totally accepted part of the criteria. And one more thing: I recommend that you indicate that you're open to trying something out of the ordinary. Maybe ask if there are any local wines that are intriguing or especially appropriate with what you're eating. This will position you as a wine lover, a seeker, and an adventurer, and just may give the sommelier the license she needs to suggest something really interesting and delicious.

What if I prefer to pick by myself?

If there is good help available, use it! But there may be times when you opt to go it alone. Say you aren't confident that the staff knows its stuff. Or say you like the challenge of picking on your own. So take a look at the list.

Some restaurants are experimenting with unique ways of presenting their wines. One I know of organizes their list by geographical latitude! Another simply plunks all their bottles on a big table, labeled with prices. But most stick with presenting a list organized by country, or by regions within a country. Some lists include a brief description of the grapes and flavors, and some restaurants are starting to organize lists by body, in which case you should be all set. But usually you'll find only a name and a vintage. So where do you start?

1. Start with the food you've chosen. Menus sometimes offer pairing suggestions. You should trust those suggestions. If the wine they claim goes with your meal sounds appealing, try it. If not? You know the drill. Think about body first and foremost. And keep an open mind about the old red–white rules.
2. Once you've narrowed down your grape options, apply your style preference. Are you in the mood for a subtle Burgundy, or a brassy California Pinot Noir? And consider going with regional matches—they're often a good bet.
3. Check out the prices. This just might help you make up your mind.
4. Take a peek at your vintage chart if you need a tie-breaker. There might be some good deals hidden in that wine list.
5. Ask the sommelier, or a knowledgeable waitperson, what she thinks of your choice. And don't let pride get in the way. If she offers another option, consider her suggestion.

What am I supposed to be looking for when she shows me the bottle?

The first thing to check is that you're getting exactly what you ordered. Make sure to check the vintage. You don't want to pay high-rated vintage prices for a lesser-rated year. If it doesn't match what you ordered, ask how it compares.

Has she told you everything you want to know about the wine? Make sure you know where it's from, maybe a little about how it's made, what grapes are in it, and what flavors it evokes. This is a great opportunity to learn something. Did she show, or tell, you how much it's going to cost you? You can ask—it's not gauche. You don't need any surprises, at least not bad ones. If she has already filled you in on everything, just nod and let her open the bottle.

She has handed me the cork. What am I supposed to do with that?

Just put it on the table. You may want to look at it for any signs of crumbling or mold, but neither necessarily means that there's anything wrong with the wine. Whatever you do, don't sniff it. All you'll get is a noseful of wet cork.

Okay. Now that she's finally poured some wine into my glass, what am I supposed to do?

Think back to what you've learned about how to taste. She served the wine, so it's your turn to see it, swirl it, smell it, sip it.

Did she pour enough for a big, healthy mouthful? If she didn't, and you are facing a stingy amount, ask for more. Remember what you learned about that first sip?

I'm always a little tempted to send it back, just to see what happens. Can I do that?

Ah, a wise guy! You're not alone. Everyone wonders about this one. Here's the deal. The sommelier or waitperson isn't really standing around waiting for you to tell her if you think the wine is tasty or not. What she's really waiting for, after you've sampled the wine, is for you to tell her if the wine is oxidized or corked. If you suspect it is, ask the sommelier or waitperson to taste it to see if she agrees.

Chances are the wine is fine. However, if the sommelier or waitperson was the one who recommended it, you should give her some feedback once you have determined that the wine isn't spoiled. Was her description accurate, in your opinion? Do you appreciate the suggestion? If—and this is a long shot—for some reason you feel that she has totally misrepresented the wine, you should tell her. Then leave it up to her to offer a replacement, or not.

What if my friend and I ordered very different foods?

Good question. One thing you can do is order different wines, by the glass. Wines by the glass are achieving new status in the restaurant world. With so many more wines available, new and easier ways to store open bottles, and customers who are curious to try new things, it makes sense for a restaurant to offer a variety of options by the glass.

Ordering by the glass makes sense if those at your table want different wines, if you want to switch wines with each course, or if you want to do some sampling. But before you order, do the math. Restaurants charge proportionately more for wine by the glass than by the bottle. As a matter of fact, the general rule of thumb is that they charge the same for one glass as they pay wholesale for the whole bottle. Talk about nice margins. A standard pour for a glass of wine is six ounces, although some restaurants pour five. A standard bottle of wine is seventy-five centiliters, or just over twenty-five ounces. That's roughly four glasses per bottle, so estimate how many glasses may be consumed and compare the cost to that of a bottle.

When ordering by the glass, don't just ask for "a glass of Chardonnay" or "some Merlot." Ask for some information about what is offered. Where is it from? What does it taste like? You can even ask to taste a little before you commit. And make sure it is poured at the table so you know what you are getting.

Another alternative that's gaining popularity is half bottles. Restaurants all over the country are beefing up their half-bottle selections. But buyer beware—half bottles are not offered at half the price. They usually go for 60 to 70 percent of the price of a full bottle, and can sometimes cost almost as much. That's because the production cost for the winery (wine excluded) is about 95 percent of that of a full bottle. But if you want more than one glass, yet less than four, and the restaurant offers a good selection by the half bottle, this may be the way to go.

Some restaurants offer carafes. These are usually measured in liter, half-liter, or quarter-liter amounts. A liter is one-third larger than a bottle. Carafes are perceived as a better value—and they are, volume-wise—but the wines offered by the carafe are usually fairly ordinary.

Sheesh. Look at this bill! I gotta ask, why does wine cost so much more at a restaurant than in a store?

I know it's sometimes infuriating. Though we are obviously willing to pay more for, say, a steak at a restaurant than we are at the butcher shop, when it comes to wine we often balk. After all, they didn't stomp those grapes in the kitchen. All they did was just open the damn bottle! But the reality is that restaurants have traditionally made a huge part of their profits on beverages. Most price wine at least double what you'd pay in a store. Some put a higher markup on affordable wines, and a lower markup on the expensive ones, so sometimes you can get a decent deal on a high-end wine, but you have to be familiar with both the wine and its retail cost to know this.

There is a heartening trend these days that actually has some restaurants lowering their margins on wine to attract business. Some are placing fixed markups on bottles, regardless of their cost.

Some are offering half-price-bottle nights, or other special promotions. It's well worth poking around to find these deals.

Why can't I just bring my own wine?

Not a bad idea. You could save a boatload of money, and you'd be guaranteed to have a wine that you want. But it depends on the restaurant. Some don't allow you to BYOB, while others are okay with it. Check before you go.

But then there's that pesky thing known as the corkage fee. Why a fee to open a bottle? For the most part, a corkage fee exists to discourage you from bringing your own bottle, and to protect the establishment from losing the revenue they've come to depend on from those markups. But don't be discouraged. Again, do the math. Corkage fees can range from about $10 to $75 a bottle. There is a chance you'll still come out ahead or at least break even, depending on the place and the wine.

The good news is that this is another area where things are looking up, at least for now. Many restaurants are scrambling for business, and some have chosen to lure customers by not charging corkage fees on certain days of the week, or with special promotions such as no corkage fees on wines from particular regions. Do some investigating. It will be worth your while.

Do I have to tip on wine?

There are those out there who make a habit of subtracting the cost of the wine before calculating a tip for their meal. That's not always a great idea. My personal opinion is that you should tip for the effort of opening and pouring, regardless of whether you brought it or bought it. If the wait staff worked with you to select the wine, reflect your appreciation in the tip. But there's no need to figure it out based on the exact cost of the bottle.

We were talking so much that we didn't finish the bottle. There's a lot left. Can I take it home with me?
That's a good, yet tricky, question. In fact, the majority of states in this country have officially legalized doggy bags for wine, or have no law on the issue one way or the other. In practice, it's another story.

In the states where it is allowed, it's usually up to the restaurant to decide whether they want to offer the take-home option or not. In many places, the regulations about resealing and repackaging the open wine before allowing it out of the restaurant are so complicated or difficult that the restaurant may choose to say no. And the rules can vary by city or county.

So the bottom line is: just ask.

THE WINERY VISIT 

There is something intoxicating about a visit to the winery: the endless rows of vines stretching down to the driveway, the fragrance of grapes fermenting in their new oak barrels, the burst of color from the roses surrounding the chateau, the buzz of bees flitting from flower to flower, the warmth of the sunlight on your arms turning to a cool caress as you cross the threshold into the soothing stone-floored tasting room.

Winery visits are one of the best ways to learn more about your personal preferences. If you have access to a tasting room, take advantage of it. Today there are more than three thousand wineries across all fifty states, with new ones popping up all the time. They are open with the hope that people just like you will come in and sample their wares. And by now you know the key to getting the most out of the experience. That's right. Communication.

When you visit a winery, don't feel like you have to know what you're talking about. Ask questions. After all, you're talking to the people who know the wine best. They welcome the opportunity to show off what they've made. Although in many cases the person in the tasting room won't actually be the winemaker or owner, he or she will be a well-informed employee whose job is specifically to talk about the wine.

Dropping In

If you're in an area where you have a choice of many places to visit, go first to the ones that intrigue you most. You'd be surprised how quickly you and your palate can burn out.

It's okay if you're drawn to familiar winery names. Just make an effort to be somewhat adventuresome while you're there, and try something they have that you've never tried before. And be sure to communicate the fact that you're a fan of the brand. Mentioning which of their wines you already like may open the door to new favorites.

Don't shy away from the smaller producers. I've come across lots of tasting rooms in Europe that look like private homes (and usually are), and I admit to having driven back and forth in front of countless dirt driveways and pacing back and forth in front of dozens of sleeping dogs while deciding whether or not to knock. Now, after more welcoming experiences than I can count, I hesitate no longer. The people who post those tasting room signs do it to get our attention. If they can't accommodate us, the worst that can happen is that they'll say no.

In some regions you'll find establishments that represent a number of local producers. This may be the way to go if you're pressed for time. Co-ops, where grapes from multiple producers are pooled to make inexpensive local wines, can also be good places to sample typical regional offerings.

Most wineries will post the hours during which they're open to the public. Some, however, conduct tastings by appointment only. Don't be turned off by that. Make an appointment! They wouldn't offer the opportunity if they didn't want visitors.

If you go during harvest time, the big wineries should have enough staff to cover, but the smaller producers will be busy, busy, busy. Stand back, smell the crush, and let them make that wine!

Tasting Fees

Many wineries, at least in this country, charge to taste—usually somewhere from $2 to $5 per person. In return, you may get a souvenir glass or the opportunity to apply the fee toward a purchase. In any case, you should expect to try something somewhat unusual in exchange for that fee—not the same-old-same-old you can find at home. And if you are charged more than $5, I sure hope you get a little something yummy to eat with those sips.

Tasting Lists

You will usually find a list of the wines being poured, some tasting notes describing the wines, and the price per bottle. See if the selection intrigues you before you commit. And you don't have to taste every wine on the list.

The Process

If you are tasting both whites and reds, you'll taste the whites first. The whites will be a little gentler on the palate, so they won't destroy your taste buds before you get to the reds. If you're tasting dessert wines, those will come last, as all that sweetness will coat the inside of your mouth, making it tough to clear the palate for other wines.

Use the water provided to rinse out your glass between the

whites, the reds, and the desserts. You can also use it to clear your palate. There should be crackers or other nibbles provided as well for that purpose.

You don't have to finish the entire amount poured into your glass. Feel free to toss the remainder into the dump bucket. And should you spit? Well, if you're planning on tasting lots of wines in one day, yes. You'll want to be alert enough to remember what you've tried!

If you have something nice to say about what you sampled, speak up. Everyone appreciates positive feedback.

The Tour

If a tour is offered, take it. At least try one. Actually seeing the process from grape to glass will help you understand the final product a lot better. An amazing bit of magic goes on there.

The Mailing List

Many wineries will offer to put you on their mailing lists, which basically means you'll get advance information on their releases and advance opportunities to buy. The benefits of this are usually some sort of savings, along with access to wines with limited quantities. In some cases, all you might be offered is a spot on the *waiting* list for the mailing list. At that point, get off the train. There's plenty more wine out there to try.

The Purchase

No purchase necessary. That's right. Don't feel pressured to buy bottles of what you've sampled. Buy only something you liked, want more of, and know you can't get at home. Ask if the wine is available at retail outlets in your area if you're not sure. Don't forget that prices in a winery are usually not bargains.

If you're tasting out of state and are interested in purchasing more than you can carry, keep in mind that some states have shipping restrictions when it comes to direct sales from wineries. Look into your home state's laws ahead of time, to avoid disappointment. If you're tasting in another country and find something you want more of, ask if it's exported. If you decide to lug some home, be aware of U.S. customs regulations. While there's no federal limit on the amount of wine you can bring back for personal use, you're required to pay duty and IRS tax on amounts over one liter. Some states limit the amount you can bring in without a license, and some apply additional state taxes. It's wise to check before you go.

And remember, when you do find something you like, no matter where you are, think about *why* you like it, and apply that information later to finding other things to try at home.

The Departure

If you have purchased and are planning to spend the rest of the day tooling around, make sure you keep the wine in the coolest part of your car. Don't put it through torture in a hot trunk before you get the chance to enjoy it. And above all, if you've been spending a good amount of time tasting, enjoying those sips to the last drop, let someone else drive.

THE JOY OF WINE BARS

One January I offered my wife a romantic winter getaway to Paris—a chance for the two of us to spend some time together after the busy holiday season at West Side Wine. Jumping at the chance for a vacation that didn't involve vineyards, she had her bags packed in a nanosecond.

Little was she aware of the trick I had up my sleeve. I was off on a wine guy's holiday, determined to check out as many of Paris's multitude of wine bars as physically possible given our six-day time limit.

After "coincidentally" coming upon five wine bars in three days, I was busted. But by the end of the week, Ellen had decided that traveling with a wine guy wasn't so bad after all. She was a wine bar convert. And why not? A little food, some local color, the chance to sample lots of unknowns, a bill that won't break the bank—what could be bad?

The definition of a wine bar, no matter what country it's in, is broad—ranging from full-scale, full-meal restaurants to café-type settings offering light bites. Whatever they are, wine bars should all have one thing in common: an exceptional variety of wines to choose from.

Here's why I love wine bars.

1. They're not bar-bars. No pounding music, no sticky floors, no beer spilled on your jacket. Most people are there for a nice, relaxed wine-related experience.
2. The quality of the wine is no doubt good. That's what wine bars are about. If they served crummy wine, what would be the point?
3. Most offer a wide range of choices, even if they specialize in one country or even one particular region. You'll find anywhere from dozens to hundreds of choices in a wine bar.
4. The best ones change their lists often, so there's always something new to try.
5. You can usually order by the bottle, glass, half glass, or flight. A flight is generally made up of three or four glasses, two to three ounces each, usually themed by region, by varietal, or by vintage.

6. You'll always find a knowledgeable staff. The wait staff and the person behind the bar are bound to be better informed than average.

There are a few things to keep in mind if you want to get the most out of a wine bar. Above all, you must communicate. Express your preferences before you decide what to try. Ask lots of questions about what is being offered. You can even ask for a custom flight, based on your preferences or your curiosity. It's best to go during off-hours if you're really going for the wine. Without the crowd, you'll get more attention. Sit at the bar if you can. This may give you the opportunity to have more of a conversation about the wine. And if you like the place, go back often. The staff will get to know you, and will likely continue to suggest new things you might want to try. Many places offer actual classes or special tastings, and sometimes bring in winemakers.

What better way to sample and learn without making a huge investment? If you have access to a good wine bar, use it.

JOINING THE CLUB

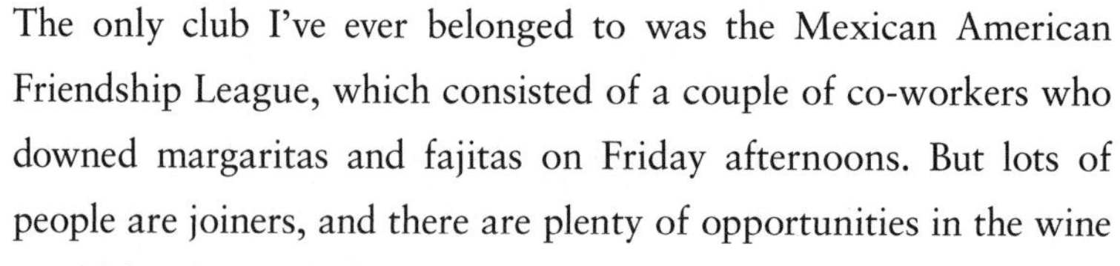

The only club I've ever belonged to was the Mexican American Friendship League, which consisted of a couple of co-workers who downed margaritas and fajitas on Friday afternoons. But lots of people are joiners, and there are plenty of opportunities in the wine world for those who are.

Wine clubs come in a few different forms. First, there are the ones run by wineries. You usually pay by the month or year, and in return for your fee you receive one or two bottles a month, or several times a year. You may also get benefits like recipes or food pairing suggestions, tasting notes or other literature, invitations to events, discounts at the winery, or VIP visits.

Is it worth it? Well, that depends. On the plus side, you may be getting access to wines that aren't available anywhere but at the winery, or before they are released to the public. If you like a certain winery, it's a good way to taste their latest offerings. And it is fun to be "surprised" by a bottle or two of wine arriving at your doorstep every so often.

On the other hand, the wine you receive will be based on what the winery chooses to send. Your personal preferences don't have a place here. How do you know that their taste will match yours? And don't forget cost. Do the math. With the shipping costs added in, are you paying more than you would, or should? Finally, speaking of shipping, you have to keep those direct sales restrictions in mind before you get too excited. Is the winery *allowed* to ship to you?

Other alternatives are the independent and retail wine clubs you can find online. They usually offer some of the benefits that the winery clubs do, without being limited to a single brand. Many offerings are themed, but again, you really have no input as to what you'll be getting. And you'll still be facing those shipping costs and restrictions.

A totally different experience exists in private wine clubs. What a great excuse for people to get together. You can do it any way you like. A theme or country or region can be put in place for each gathering, and every "member" can bring a bottle to share with the group. One Saturday I had the challenge of helping four different customers, each apparently going to the same party, each looking to win the prize for bringing the best Rioja. Luckily, I carried four equally good ones.

At wine clubs sometimes fees are collected, and a designated host is responsible for picking all the wines. Some tasting groups use their strength in numbers to pool orders, so they can benefit from case discounts without having to buy an entire case. Others actually require members to bring a solid case (all one wine) to each meeting, where exchanges are made and everyone ends up with a mixed case to take home.

Many private wine clubs have been going on for years, with many friendships, and even romances, blossoming over the glass. Can you think of a better way to further your wine education?

SOCIAL STUDIES 

Imagine being invited to a huge outdoor party on a sunny autumn afternoon. You're surrounded by lovely scenery—perhaps a lush valley, golden hilltops, or miles and miles of vines. There's live music playing, and children are dancing around in a dizzying frenzy. The smell of local delicacies wafts through the air. Across the way, artists are proudly displaying their masterpieces. Craftspeople have spread out their wares. Best of all, there are hundreds of glasses of wine at your disposal. And the party could last for days.

Well, guess what? You are invited. Wine festivals are one of the many wine-related events that are open to the public. Sometimes combined with food festivals, they can also be called fairs or expos, and are a great excuse for a vacation. They most often occur near where the grapes are grown, which usually means a beautiful part of the world, along with some pretty nice accommodations and dining experiences nearby. And be prepared for the local winemakers to talk your ear off! It's great fun.

Entry is usually available via daily or weekend passes. Check your local papers for events in your area, and go online to see what's going on in the rest of the world.

Industry tastings are one of my favorite things about being the Wine Guy. And no, it's not because of the free drinks. It's because being in a huge room full of winemakers allows me the opportunity to witness their passion firsthand, to hear from the horses' mouths what they want their wines to express. And there is no other place to find such variety under one roof. It's almost overwhelming, even for me.

But you don't have to change your life and go into the business like I did to have access to this experience. Some industry tastings are open to the public during designated hours, usually at night, usually for a fee. They may be sponsored by a specific trade group, such as the New Zealand Winegrowers. Check your local paper's event or food-and-wine section for listings.

There are plenty of other types of wine events geared toward the public, such as charity fundraisers, singles gatherings, and winemaker dinners hosted by restaurants. All fun, all informative. You can find thousands of listings online, at localwineevents.com.

Many retail locations bring in winemakers or their representatives for in-store tastings. I offer tastings every weekend. Mine are free, but there are some states that prohibit freebies in a retail venue. If your favorite shop conducts tastings, take advantage of them. And if you prefer a more intimate setting, ask your wine seller if he or she ever participates in private tastings, or knows someone who does. If you're willing to let a few friends in on the act, it can make for a nice party.

Need a more structured approach to learning? Formal wine classes are available just about everywhere. Ask your wine seller for recommendations.

PARTY ON!

Every summer, come rain or shine, Ellen and I throw a wine party. Not a formal "tasting" event, just a down-and-dirty, drop-on-by, more-the-merrier, raucous party. It just happens to be somewhat about the wine.

So where do we start? Where do you think? I pick a country or region and choose about four or five different reds, four or five different whites, rosés if appropriate, sometimes a bubbly or two, and at least one dessert wine that all fit the theme. Since it is a wine party, I have more on hand than I normally would for a dinner party.

Once I've settled on the wine, I print out copies of the list. These I leave on a table near the wine, with some pencils, for those who want to keep track of what they've tried.

Plenty of glasses are key. People put them down, forget them, or want to use different glasses for different wines. Sturdy four-ounce "tasting" glasses are ideal. I've found them at a good price in bulk, and they've been well worth the investment.

For food, we go with anything that even remotely relates to the region. Tapas with Spanish wines. Shrimp with Australian wines. Pigs in a blanket and mini-burgers with American wines. The important thing is to serve bite-sized finger food. Balancing a plate and utensils along with a glass is tricky. We make sure there is plenty of food so there's no need for anyone to rush out to dinner afterward.

That's it. I just open a bottle of each wine, leave the others on the table (with some whites in reserve on ice) with a corkscrew, and let everyone help themselves. With an instant common topic ("What are you trying?"), the crowd starts to mingle early and always tends to stay late.

And the party gets bigger and bigger every year. It's already wall-to-wall. Wine has a way of bringing in a crowd and keeping it lively. Just ask my neighbors.

One thing's for sure: being the Wine Guy has done wonders for my popularity, especially at parties. It now seems as though everyone wants to talk to me. Some people want free advice. Some are particularly intrigued by the fact that I've chucked it all to follow my passion. But all seem curious about what it's actually like to do what I do.

One thing is certain: it's very different from everything I've ever done before. Take, for instance, my anonymity, which I used to treasure. Now I can't take a walk through the neighborhood or to the park without at least five people waving to me and shouting out a hello, or a dog recognizing me and sniffing at my pockets for treats. My wife calls me the mayor of the Upper West Side. And, surprising to me, I like it.

Then there's the issue of owning my own business. Back when I was a TV guy, I made a point of leaving my work at the office. I rarely even watched television when I got home. Now my work is always on my mind. Like during dinner, as I'm sampling a wonderful new Riesling, or when I'm on vacation, barreling through rows of Chenin Blanc in some French winemaker's Range Rover.

And let's not forget the privacy thing. I used to have a secretary barring the way to my office—my own personal first line of defense. Now my door's always wide open, and *anybody* can just walk right in. Like the time one of my favorite writers stopped by to pick up a bottle of Zinfandel. And when I found myself face-to-face across the counter from one of the greatest jazz pianists ever. I've made lots of interesting new friends in the past few years.

So I guess, all in all, I have to say life as the Wine Guy is good. Being around wine makes me happy. Being around people who are into wine makes me happy, too. And the people who make me happiest are my regular customers, the people I see every day. We've been through a lot together. I've been privy to their engagements and the details of their weddings, have been there to congratulate them on their promotions, and have lent a sympathetic ear when they've had a bad day at work. I've lived vicariously through their vacations. I've helped them pick out Champagne to celebrate the births of their children, and I've started to see those children grow up.

But we've also been through something else together. We've learned from each other just what it takes to make this whole wine thing a pleasurable and rewarding experience—from both sides of the counter.

I've learned to recognize the obstacles people face, and I've seen just how obstructive those obstacles can be. As a result, I've learned how important it is to get people to open up.

I'm sure my incessant questioning has been a pain in the ass to many of my customers. And deciphering their responses has at times been a challenge to me. But we have both learned to be patient with each other.

Most important, my customers have taught me how to listen. And in exchange, they've been exposed to a whole new way of thinking about wine.

And we're all still learning together. There's always a new vintage to try, an unknown winemaker's wares to sample, an up-and-coming grape to explore. Wine is a topic that never gets old.

Have I been successful with my business venture? Fortunately, yes. But to me, the real success is measured by what I've seen happen with my customers. They've returned, week after week, each time a little more relaxed, a little more confident, a little more communicative, and a lot more adventuresome.

And you know what? We're all having a lot more fun.

A professor stood before his philosophy class with some items in front of him. When the class began, he wordlessly picked up a very large, empty mayonnaise jar and proceeded to fill it with golf balls. He then asked the students if the jar was full. They agreed it was.

The professor then picked up a box of pebbles and poured them into the jar. He shook the jar lightly. The pebbles, of course, rolled into the open areas between the golf balls. He asked the students again if the jar was full. They agreed it was.

Next, the professor picked up a box of sand and poured it into the jar. Of course the sand filled up the remaining space. He then asked once more if the jar was full. The students responded with a unanimous, "YES!"

The professor then produced two glasses of wine from under the table and proceeded to pour the entire contents into the jar, effectively filling the empty spaces between the grains of sand. The students laughed. "Now," said the professor, as the laughter subsided, "I want you to recognize that this jar represents your life. The golf balls are the important things—your family, your partner, your health, your children, your friends, your favorite passions—things that if everything else was lost and only they remained would keep your life full.

"The pebbles are the other things that matter, like your job, your house, your car.

"The sand is everything else, the small stuff. If you put the sand into the jar first," he continued, "there is no room for the pebbles or the golf balls. The same goes for your life: if you spend all your time and energy on the small stuff, you will never have room for the things that are important to you.

"Pay attention to the things that are critical to your happiness. Play with your children. Take care of your health. Take your partner out dancing. Play another eighteen holes.

"There will always be time to go to work, clean the house, give a dinner party, and wash the dishes. Take care of the golf balls first—the things that really matter. Set your priorities. The rest is just sand."

One of the students raised her hand and inquired what the wine represented.

The professor smiled. "I'm glad you asked. It just goes to show you that no matter how full your life may seem, there's always room for a couple of glasses of wine."

WHAT AM I DRINKING?

Someone brings you a special bottle that you flip over. But you can't figure out what grape or grapes it's made from. The information is not on the label. It might be an Old World wine, named after the region in which it's made. Or maybe the grape is listed on the label, but you never realized that *was* the name of a grape. Then again, maybe it's a blend you're not familiar with.

Take the easy route. Just figure out what country the wine is from, then use this chart.

It would be impossible to cover every single appellation, obscure grape, or mysterious blend, so I've stuck with a good representation of the wines you're most likely to come across. Be aware that some of the wines included are blends of many different grapes. In those cases, I've listed only the major grapes involved. Also know that not all of the grapes listed next to a particular region will be used in every wine produced there. There are variations; I've shown the primary grapes from which the winemakers within those regions pick and choose.

FRENCH WHITES

REGION/WINE	GRAPES
ALSATIAN	Pinot Blanc, Riesling, Pinot Auxerrois, Gewürztraminer, Muscat, Pinot Gris, Sylvaner
BEAUJOLAIS	Chardonnay
BORDEAUX: Graves, Sauternes, Pessac-Léognan	Sauvignon Blanc, Semillon, Muscadelle
BURGUNDY: Pouilly-Fuissé, Puligny-Montrachet, Chassagne-Montrachet, Chablis, Mâcon	Chardonnay
LOIRE VALLEY: Sancerre, Pouilly-Fumé, Quincy, Touraine	Sauvignon Blanc
Vouvray, Montlouis, Chinon, Saumur, Anjou, Savennières	Chenin Blanc
MUSCADET	Melon de Bourgogne
RHONE (NORTHERN): Hermitage, Crozes-Hermitage, St-Joseph, St-Péray	Marsanne, Roussanne
Condrieu	Viognier
RHONE (SOUTHERN): Côtes du Rhône, Châteauneuf-du-Pape	Viognier, Marsanne, Roussanne

FRENCH REDS

REGION/WINE	GRAPES
ALSATIAN	Pinot Noir
BEAUJOLAIS: Brouilly, Chénas, Chiroubles, Côte de Brouilly, Fleurie, Julienas, Morgon, Moulin-à-Vent, Régnié, St-Amour	Gamay
BORDEAUX: St-Emilion, Pomerol	Mostly Merlot with Cabernet Sauvignon, Cabernet Franc
St-Estèphe, Margaux, St-Julien, Pauillac, Graves, Médoc, Haut-Médoc, Pessac-Léognan	Mostly Cabernet Sauvignon with Merlot and Cabernet Franc
BURGUNDY: Chambolle-Musigny, Volnay, Pommard, Vosne-Romainée, Gevrey-Chambertin, Eschezaux	Pinot Noir
LOIRE VALLEY: Sancerre	Pinot Noir
Chinon, Saumur, Borgeuil, Anjou	Cabernet Franc, Gamay
RHÔNE (NORTHERN): Hermitage, Crozes-Hermitage, Cornas, St-Joseph, Côte-Rôtie	Syrah, Viognier
RHÔNE (SOUTHERN): Châteauneuf-du-Pape, Vacqueyras, Gigondas, Côtes du Rhône-Villages, Côtes du Rhône	Grenache, Syrah, Mourvèdre, Cinsault

ITALIAN WHITES

REGION/WINE	GRAPES
CAMPANIA: Greco di Tufo	Greco di Tufo
Fiano d' Avellino	Fiano
MARCHES: Verdicchio	Verdicchio, Trebbiano, Malvasia
PIEDMONT: Asti Spumante	Moscato (Muscat)
Muscato d'Asti	Moscato
Gavi	Cortese
Roero	Arneis
TUSCANY: Vernaccia di San Gimignano	Vernaccia
Vin Santo and other Tuscan whites	Trebbiano
UMBRIA: Orvieto	Trebbiano, Malvasia, Verdicchio, Verdello
VENETO: Pinot Grigio	Pinot Gris
Soave	Garganega, Trebbiano, Chardonnay
Prosecco	Prosecco

ITALIAN REDS

REGION/WINE	GRAPES
APULIA (PUGLIA): Salice Salentino	Negroamaro, Primitivo
Primitivo	Primitivo
CAMPANIA: Taurasi	Aglianico
PIEDMONT: Barolo	Nebbiolo
Barbaresco	Nebbiolo
Barbera	Barbera
Dolcetto	Dolcetto
Gattinara	Nebbiolo, Bonarda
UMBRIA: Sagrantino di Montefalco	Sagrantino
Rosso di Montelfalco	Sagrantino, Sangiovese, Trebbiano
VENETO: Valpolicella, Amarone, Bardolino	Corvina, Rondinella, Molinara

NORTH AMERICAN

WINE	GRAPES
Meritage—Red	Cabernet Sauvignon, Merlot, Cabernet Franc, Petit Verdot, Malbéc
Meritage—White	Sauvignon Blanc, Semillon

PORTUGUESE WHITES

WINE	GRAPES
Vinho Verde	Arinto, Alvarinho, Trajadura

PORTUGUESE REDS

REGION/WINE	GRAPES
Dão	Touriga Nacional, Tinta Roriz (Tempranillo), Bastardo
Duoro	Touriga Nacional, Tinta Roriz

SPANISH WHITES

REGION/WINE	GRAPES
Cava	Xarel-lo, Macabéo (Viura), Parellada, Chardonnay
Rias Baixas	Albariño
Rioja	Viura
Rueda	Verdejo, Sauvignon Blanc, Viura

SPANISH REDS

REGION/WINE	GRAPES
Jumilla	Monastrell, Cabernet Sauvignon, Tempranillo (Cencibel)
Priorato	Grenache, Cabernet Sauvignon, Syrah, Carignan
Ribera de Duero	Tempranillo (Tinta del País), Grenache
Rioja	Tempranillo, Grenache

WHAT MAKES WHAT?

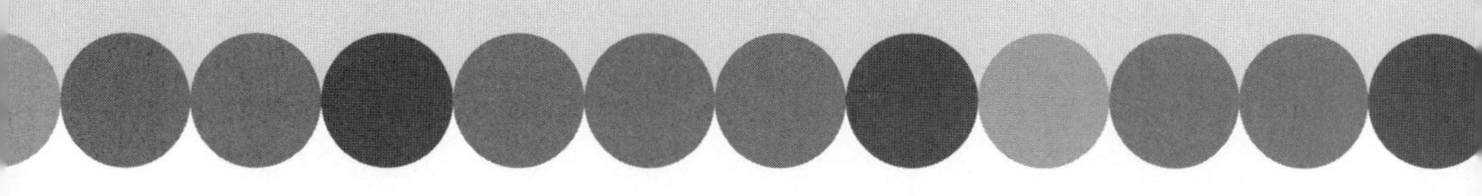

Do you know which of the Everydays and Breakaways you like, but have trouble remembering what wines they make besides the ones named after the grapes themselves? With this chart, there's no problem.

Obviously, this is by no means a complete list. Besides varietals (wines named after the dominant grape used), there are many more wines made with these grapes. In some blends, you will find the grapes listed somewhere on the label; in others, you won't. But here are some places where you're likely to find your faves. Use the previous chart as a reference to specific appellations.

THESE GRAPES	MAKE THESE WINES
WHITES	
Albariño	Albariño
Chardonnay	White Burgundy, White Beaujolais
Chenin Blanc	Vouvray, Montlouis, Saumur, Savennières, Chinon

THESE GRAPES	MAKE THESE WINES
Gewürztraminer	Just Gewürztraminer . . . that's it!
Grüner Veltliner	Grüner is Grüner . . . nothing else
Pinot Gris	Pinot Grigio
Riesling	Alsatian white blends
Sauvignon Blanc	Some white Loires (Sancerre, Pouilly-Fumé, Touraine, Quincy), white Bordeaux blends, white Meritage blends
Viognier	Condrieu, white Côtes du Rhône, white Châteauneuf-du-Pape
REDS	
Cabernet Franc	Most red Loires (e.g., Chinon, Saumur, Bourgueuil, Anjou), red Bordeaux blends, Meritage blends
Cabernet Sauvignon	Red Bordeaux blends, Meritage blends, Tuscan blends
Dolcetto	Dolcetto d'Alba, Dolcetto d'Asti
Gamay	Beaujolais, Loire red blends
Grenache	Garnacha (Spain), Southern Rhône red blends, Languedoc red blends
Malbéc	Cahors

THESE GRAPES	MAKE THESE WINES
Merlot	Red Bordeaux blends, Meritage blends, Tuscan blends
Nebbiolo	Barolo, Barbaresco, Gattinara, Ghemme
Pinotage	Just Pinotage
Pinot Noir	Red Burgundy, Red Sancerre, Alsatian reds
Sangiovese	Tuscan reds
Syrah	Northern Rhône reds, Southern Rhône red blends, Languedoc red blends
Tempranillo	Rioja, Ribera del Duero, Portuguese red blends
Touriga Nacional	Touriga Nacional
Zinfandel	Primitivo

INDEX

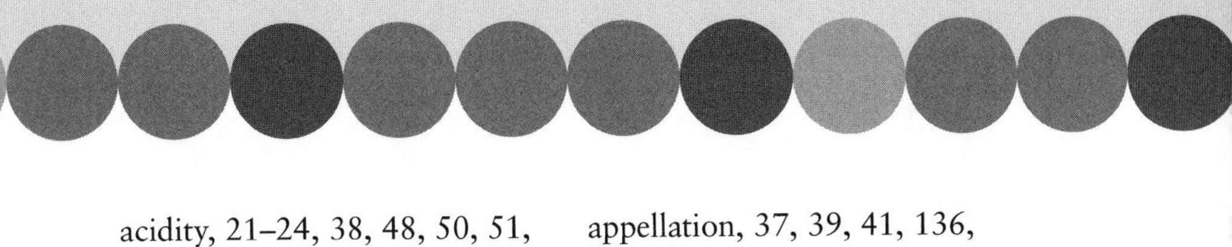